Read One
Each Day

100 Days
to Your
Breakthrough

Your miracle starts with a breakthrough.
100 devotional messages and prayers to
help you break through spiritually to see
your desires and dreams come to pass.

Jeanne Alcott

LifeRich Publishing is a registered trademark of The Reader's Digest Association, Inc.

This book is a work of non-fiction. Unless otherwise noted, the author and the publisher make no explicit guarantees as to the accuracy of the information contained in this book and in some cases, names of people and places have been altered to protect their privacy.

LifeRich Publishing books may be ordered through booksellers or by contacting:

LifeRich Publishing
1663 Liberty Drive
Bloomington, IN 47403
www.liferichpublishing.com
1 (888) 238-8637

Because of the dynamic nature of the Internet, any web addresses or links contained in this book may have changed since publication and may no longer be valid. The views expressed in this work are solely those of the author and do not necessarily reflect the views of the publisher, and the publisher hereby disclaims any responsibility for them.

Any people depicted in stock imagery provided by Getty Images are models, and such images are being used for illustrative purposes only.
Certain stock imagery © Getty Images.

All Scripture quotations, unless otherwise indicated, are taken from the Amplified Bible, Copyright © 1954, 1958, 1962, 1964, 1965, 1987 by The Lockman Foundation. Used by permission.

Scripture quotations marked MSG are taken from THE MESSAGE, copyright © 1993, 2002, 2018 by Eugene H. Peterson. Used by permission of NavPress. All rights reserved. Represented by Tyndale House Publishers, Inc.

Scripture quotations marked (NLT) are taken from the Holy Bible, New Living Translation, copyright ©1996, 2004, 2015 by Tyndale House Foundation. Used by permission of Tyndale House Publishers, Inc., Carol Stream, Illinois 60188. All rights reserved.

Scripture taken from the New Century Version®. Copyright © 2005 by Thomas Nelson. Used by permission. All rights reserved.

The Scripture quotations marked "Moffatt" are taken from *The Bible, James Moffatt Translation* by James A. R. Moffatt. Copyright © 1922, 1924, 1925, 1926, 1935 by Harper Collins San Francisco. Copyright © 1950, 1952, 1953, 1954 by James A. R. Moffatt. Published in 1994 under special arrangement with Harper Collins San Francisco by Kregel Publications, a division of Kregel, Inc., P.O. Box 2607, Grand Rapids, MI 49501.

The Scripture quotations marked (NEB) are taken from *The New English Bible*. Copyright © the Delegates of the Oxford University Press and the Syndics of the Cambridge University Press 1961, 1970.

ISBN: 978-1-4897-2396-3 (sc)
ISBN: 978-1-4897-2397-0 (hc)
ISBN: 978-1-4897-2398-7 (e)

Library of Congress Control Number: 2019909894

Print information available on the last page.

LifeRich Publishing rev. date: 07/23/2019

Introduction

The Lord has broken through my enemies before me, like the bursting out of great waters. So he called the name of that place Baal-perazim [Lord of breaking through] (II Samuel 5:20).

How can you get a breakthrough to something for which you have been waiting? You know those times when you can't seem to get the answer you need or see the fulfillment to a desire or vision you have.

As soon as you started praying about a need or challenge in your life, you were heard in heaven. God hears the beating of your heart, the thoughts in your mind. However, as you well know, the answer does not always come immediately. Why is that? What's going on with heaven while you wait?

This is what the man Daniel in the Bible was wondering. He was praying because a vision had been given to him that showed war was coming to Israel. That concerned him so much that he began to fast and pray asking God if his people would be victorious. He wanted to know what their destiny would be.

For three weeks, he continued to pray and seek God. In other words, he was staying connected until he got an answer. At the end of those days, an angel appeared to him and said, *O Daniel, you greatly beloved man, fear not for from the first day that you set your mind and heart to understand and to humble yourself before your God, your words were heard, and I have come in response to your words. But the prince of the kingdom of Persia withstood me for twenty-one days. Then Michael, one of the chief [of the celestial] princes, came to help me, for I remained there with the kings of Persia* (Daniel 10:12, 13).

As soon as Daniel started praying, he was heard in heaven. But he was on hold because hindering spirits were holding back his answer. So he had to get a breakthrough.

As you are on hold, waiting for God's answers, be as Daniel. Stay connected. Continue to pray and believe. Seek God.

You must pray against hindering spirits that try to stop your answer just as the spirit forces were stopping Daniel's answer. Your warfare is not with just physical opponents, but it's with the powers that are in the supernatural realm—the spirit forces of darkness. (Ref. Ephesians 6.)

As Daniel continued to pray, God's forces defeated Satan's forces in a mighty way. That's what happens when you stay connected and don't give up when you're on hold. As you pray and stand in faith, God's forces are responding and being sent out. They will overcome the wicked forces that are working against you. Those hindering spirits will be defeated. Then when God's timing is right, the answer can be released. You can receive your miracle breakthrough.

See why it's so important to stay connected? If you hang up, and you stop seeking and believing, then why should the divine forces of God continue to work for you? You've given up and walked away, so they walk away. Why should they keep warring against what's against you?

Don't call off the warfare by walking away. Allow God's forces to keep working for you and crush those hindering spirits by staying connected with His power. Refuse to give up just as Daniel did. Go after all God has for you and believe you will have a breakthrough. How can you miss with the kind of powerful forces sent from heaven to do warfare in your behalf? You can't miss it unless you disconnect.

This book can help you stay connected to God's power until you get your breakthrough. Every miracle starts with a breakthrough. You can get a breakthrough in your health. A good break in your job or with your finances. I've had ministry Partners tell me how exciting it was when a special needs child had a breakthrough in their activities and abilities. Others have seen it happen when a family member was turned around. There have been miracle breakthroughs in finding a spouse, having the ability to have children, or being healed from a relationship issue. What has not worked in the past can start working now. There are wonders of every kind waiting for you. Now pray God's will into your life by faith.

See something good happen in that legal problem, in trying to learn something new, or navigate tough issues. Watch as your dream HAPPENS! You can see all God has for you come to pass. So for the next 100 days, take this challenge to read a devotional and prayer from this book each day. One hundred is a number showing COMPLETENESS. Each devotional and prayer holds a specific piece to your breakthrough. Believe your breakthrough will begin and God will be able to complete what He wants to do in your situation.

We are not guaranteeing a miracle in 100 days. But we believe if you live by the principles of the Word of God in these messages each day, you can see the start of your miracle

So are you ready to start breaking through into the spiritual realm where your miracle is? Then let's get started. And be sure to use the NOTES section to write down what's happening to you as God moves on your life. That will help you realize what is happening over time. There's just something about seeing your thoughts and feelings written down. And even if things don't look good for awhile, stay connected to God's power through His Word and prayers in this book.

We are here to pray with you so share with us what you're believing for and we will come into a prayer of agreement with you according to Matthew 18:19. Just write to: Jeanne and John Alcott, PO Box 3400, Broken Arrow, OK 74013, or call 918-459-9191 or go to our Web site at www.AlcottMinistries@cox.net. We are here waiting to hear from you and stand in faith for your miracle! Also, it's important to share with us your praise report of what God does.

Jeanne Alcott

Remove the Limitations

When you remove what limits your thinking and your faith, that's when you release the power potential for your breakthrough.

Day 1

You've Just Scratched the Surface

God's encouraging word to you today is this—what you have seen happen so far is just the beginning of what He is doing.

The small step you have taken is only the start toward where He's taking you.

The small blessing you have experienced is simply a starter to the big blessings coming.

The way you have seen God begin to move in your behalf is just that—it's only the beginning. Greater and mightier things are to come. You have just scratched the surface.

There's so much more to see. There is a sign like this in front of the National Archives building in Washington DC. These archives hold important documents such as the Constitution and Bill of Rights. Documents that tell of the beginning of this nation and of the foundation of greatness God established. Then in front of the National Archives is a statue that has these words engraved on it: *What Is Past Is Prologue.* One day a tourist saw the statue and asked their cab driver what the sign meant. And their response was, "It means, 'Brother, you ain't seen nothin' yet!'"

All the good things which have happened in the past were just the beginning. The prologue. The introduction to what God is going to do. He wants to show you the great and mighty things to come for your life. There are much more impressive miracles, answers, and accomplishments God has ready to do for you.

The past of what you've seen is just a prologue to what can happen. Now God wants you to believe for those greater and mightier things to come to you. Prepare your heart and mind to be open to receive them. Remove limited thinking and believing.

In Jeremiah, the Lord invites us and challenges us to do this: *Call to Me and I will answer you and show you great and mighty things, fenced in and hidden, which you do not know (do not distinguish and recognize, have knowledge of and understand)* (Jeremiah 33:3).

He wants you to call for great and mighty things! In other words, expect your God to show you what He can do! When He says *great* things He means enormous, huge, big beyond "your big." And when He says *mighty*, He means He's going to do something impressive. Grand. It will have force behind it.

You have just seen the beginning of what is to come. Believe that and begin to ask for greater and mightier things to happen. Call for them. Meaning, name them. Tell God what you are believing for Him to do. Call to Him, and He'll answer you and show you great and mighty things that have been fenced in, meaning held back from you. There's been a fence between you and your desired answer. You haven't been able to see those things come forth into your life. They've been hidden.

You've waited and you've watched, you've worked and you have prayed, but where are those greater and mightier things? That's what God is about to show you. He doesn't want you to stop at the beginning of what you've seen but go on into the deeper work that He can do for you.

Don't limit the Lord to what you have at this time, but be watching and waiting for something greater. Something mightier. You haven't seen anything yet. You've just been introduced to the power of God. You have just tasted His goodness. There's a big meal waiting for you to experience and eat of all the good things He has.

Go around with a mindset and a heart-determination that says, *I will experience the greater and mightier things God has for me. This is just the beginning!*

Envision favor and blessing and promotion. Picture greater health. An increased sense of His presence and the power of His Spirit. You can have revival in that relationship. Your finances can be revived. What's going on in your work or business or ministry—expect for the wind of the Holy Spirit to blow in and do great and mighty things. This is for your marriage and children and your house and transportation and all that God intends for your life.

You have just scratched the surface of what has been prepared. So believe this is only the beginning of what God is going to do for everything on your heart.

A Spiritual Powerline to say out loud:
"I CALL FOR GREATER AND MIGHTIER THINGS!"

A powerful prayer to pray:
Lord, today I am calling to You. I want to see the greater and mightier things that You've prepared for me. So I set my faith to experience what is to come. I'm ready! In the name of Jesus. Amen.

NOTES:

_____

_____

_____

Day 2

I Want To

The promises God makes in His Word are not there for us just to read and feel good about. They are there for us to *receive!* So when we pray, we should pray according to those promises.

My husband, John, was just reminding me of how he did this in our life when we needed a new home. This was before we were in full-time ministry, and we had come to a point that our current home was not meeting our needs, so we began searching around town for what was available.

As we searched, we found one house that we thought was wonderful. It seemed as though it would be just right for what we needed. So we began to pray about it, but after awhile John felt as if maybe it was *too* wonderful. Now, to some people it wouldn't be, but to him it was. You know how you can want something so much, but it's almost as though you don't dare ask for something that wonderful. An amazing healing, a successful career, or a loving and caring spouse. A financial blessing, a promotion, a unified family, or a quick resolution to a problem. Some things just seem too wonderful to receive!

So as we were praying about this, one day on the way home from work, John was talking to the Lord about this type of house. He came to the place where he opened up his heart in an honest way and said to Him, "I believe You *can* provide that kind of home for us, but I don't believe You *want* to." In other words, he was saying that it was too much to hope that God would provide something such as that.

Later that evening at home, he was watching a religious program and a guest minister was on it. As this minister began to share, he told the story in the Bible of the leper who came to Jesus to be healed. He rushed up to Jesus and begged Him on his knees saying, *If You are willing, You are able to make me clean. And being moved with pity and sympathy, Jesus reached out His hand and touched him, and said to him, I am willing; be made clean! And at once the leprosy [completely] left him and he was made clean [by being healed]* (Mark 1:40-42).

Then this minister went on to say, "Many believers have faith that God *can* do something, but they don't believe He *wants* to. They're unsure if God desires to do it for them even though they believe He is all-powerful."

John just stopped in his tracks. He knew God was speaking right to his heart, because he had just said those words to the Lord. "I believe You can provide that kind of home for us, but I don't believe You want to." He realized he was being just as the leper who came to Jesus and said, "I know you can make me whole if You are willing." And what was the response from Jesus? "I am! Receive the healing I have for you." The leper received and was made whole.

John knew God *could* provide the home we needed, and now he was going to change what he was saying to show he believed God also *would* provide it. So he began to pray the promise from the Word. **He was praying the "I-want-to" promise.**

God has that same promise for you. The "I-want-to" promise. He is not just able, but desires to do it for you.

So we began to pray the promise and believe God's Word that He would provide in His timing and His way and in His will. We discovered a vacant lot for sale in that same housing addition and purchased it. Eventually we built a home that met our needs and blessed us. It was in that home that I began a Bible study and birthed Alcott Ministries. See, God knew what was about to be born into our lives and that we would need this home, and also He just wanted to bless us with the house.

God has amazing blessings planned for you. And they become possible when you pray the promises. That's when your prayers produce power. So believe today that God not only *can* but *wants* to bless you in the area where you have need. Then as you pray, expect to receive!

A Spiritual Powerline to say out loud:
"GOD WANTS TO DO THIS FOR ME!"

A powerful prayer to pray:
Lord, I believe what You are speaking to my heart right now. You not only can do this for me, but You want to! So I pray this promise from Your Word today. Now, I expect to receive what You

have planned for my life and those around me. You are sending blessing! In the name of Jesus. Amen.

NOTES:

_____

_____

_____

Day 3

How Big Is God to You

When we are facing difficulties or striving for what we desire, we can feel things are too big for us. During this time, I imagine that God would like to wave His hand in front of our face to remind us of how big He is. That's because when we see the size of God, nothing can stop us from overcoming and moving forward into what He has for us.

This is the message He gave to the Israelites, and they got it! They were facing a big opportunity to gain something that would be great for them. Before them was a land that was prosperous and they had a choice—they could call that land their home after being in the wilderness for forty years, or they could turn around and go back into the wilderness. Seems an easy choice. Why would they turn back? Because they were facing the Jordan River and it was at flood stage and going across it was the only way to get where they wanted to go.

On top of that, Joshua was now the new leader because Moses had passed away.

So they had a new person as the head of all the Israelites.

Plus the people were a new generation.

So they weren't around when God performed the big miracle of parting the Red Sea.

Now, they were trying to get to their new homes with their families.

But they were facing a swollen river that had a strong and rapid current because the winter snows in the mountain had melted into the river.

What's happening? **The devil is showing his size!** Through those scary raging circumstances, he appears to be bigger than what God can do for them. He's trying to take what is theirs.

How many times does the devil try to show you his size? As you view the circumstances around you, do things appear bigger than God to you? If so, that's when the devil will be able to take what is yours. Get your eyes on God through His Word and see again how big He is. He's going to show you how to **move ahead and take your victory!**

So God told the priests to carry the Ark of the Covenant which represents His presence and power being with them. Then they walked right up to the brink of the river and stood there with all the people behind them. The priests were to be the first ones to put their feet into the waters. So there they were—facing this cold rapid river at flood stage. They are at the point that if they're going to win the place promised to them, they're going to have to recognize the size of God.

That's where you are right now. God knows you're facing some things that are making you feel as though all you can do is turn back. **You're at the point that if you're going to win the desire in your heart and overcome the problems in your path, you will have to recognize the size of God.** See how big He is compared to the cold raging river you're facing.

Joshua and the people believed their God was bigger than what they were facing. So the priests stepped into that muddy river and all of a sudden the streams of melted snow that were flowing dried up. They were cut off. Soon the river receded and became dry. Dry! Almost two million people walked across on dry ground and went on to have victory over their enemies. They took possession of their new homes and the blessings God had for them.

Oh! Feel victory coming on. You're about to move ahead and take it! Take possession of what God has for you as He rewards you for your faith. When you recognize the size of the One within you, that's when you will not fear what the devil is doing, because you know what your Father can do.

You know how big God is in you so you're going to win. What you've been standing there waiting for and believing for will now be yours. You have victory!

A Spiritual Powerline to say out loud:
"MY GOD IS BIGGER!"

A powerful prayer to pray:
Lord, even though the challenge in front of me seems bigger than what I can handle, I know it's not bigger than You. And Your presence and power are in my spirit. I see You as BIG today. And You're moving on my behalf. So I take my victory in the name of Jesus. Amen.

NOTES:

_____

_____

_____

Day 4

Concentrate on Climbing

A father was telling the story of how his five-year-old son, Aaron, decided he wanted to climb a large tree they had in their backyard. So he decided to teach him how he could do it safely.

I think of how the Father God does that. We find a mountain that we want to climb—it's something we want to see accomplished. So the Lord comes to teach us how and strengthens us to do it. But sometimes what happens to us is what happened to this boy—when we start the climb, fear tries to take over. The fear of falling.

Aaron began to whine, "I'm going to fall. I'm going to fall." So his dad tried to coach him along and told him to move from the branch to the center of the tree. But all he could concentrate on was falling. He kept whining. "I'm going to fall." Can you hear yourself saying that as a kid—a grown-up kid. "Oh Lord, I'm trying to do this but it isn't working. I tried to climb to see this desire fulfilled, but it's not happening. Things are going wrong. I'm going to fall."

God tries to talk to us and encourage our spirit to keep climbing, but it's hard to hear Him above our whining! So He does what Aaron's dad did; He gets our attention with a word to us. The dad said, "Aaron! Don't think about falling; think about climbing!" As soon as the boy started thinking about climbing to get up the tree, his fear vanished, and he made it! He was able to do what he wanted.

Just as that son, we need to concentrate on climbing—not concentrate on falling. God knows we may have some fear that things are not going to go the way we want, but still we have to put the whining aside and keep climbing. **Focus upwards—where we** want to be. Know that we have God's strength within us and He will make sure this is completed.

Hebrews 13:21 promises you this. God will *strengthen (complete, perfect) and make you what you ought to be and equip you with everything good that you may carry out His will; [while He Himself] works in you and accomplishes that which is pleasing in His sight, through Jesus Christ (the Messiah).*

He's going to give you so much strength that you will be fully equipped to complete what you need to do. In other words, you're going to have everything you need to make it up that mountain. He equips you with everything good so that you can carry out His will.

It's His will for you to rise above debt or financial need. It's God's will for you to have good relationships and the friends you desire. He wants you to scale that mountain concerning being happy in where you live and what you do. You're going to see this thing completed in your life.

You will see that situation restored. You'll be victorious in losing that weight or changing that habit or getting a promotion. You suffered through and kept climbing to see your family get closer together, to get that home you needed. He strengthens you as you ask Him to help you complete your quest to grow spiritually, to witness to another person, or help someone in their life. By faith, you are willing to keep climbing until you see something completed. You go to a new level in your life.

Listen, you never stop climbing! You just trust *while* you're doing it! You've been climbing toward better health, and God can help you complete that climb. You're scrambling to get something going on your job or in a life-project that's important to you—believe it is going to be completed. God can give you the strength to keep scrambling. Concentrate on climbing and focus upwards.

A Spiritual Powerline to say out loud:
"I'M GOING TO KEEP CLIMBING!"

A powerful prayer to pray:
Lord, I'm going to keep climbing. I will make it to what I desire, and I'll do it by Your strength. So, I trust You as I climb. I focus upwards. And I know I'm going to see Your work completed in my life. In the name of Jesus. Amen.

NOTES:

_____

_____

_____

Day 5

Break Past the Barrier

No one denies that there are times when something comes to shake us up. It tries to ruffle or disturb us. The circumstances can cause us to become unnerved.

To get to the place where life is smooth again, sometimes we have to break through the shaking time. And we can only break past that barrier by being steadfast in our faith.

But here's the problem—every time we start to use our faith, the shaking gets worse! This is how the devil works. If you're getting too near what he knows will help you or bless your life or fulfill you, then he makes the shaking much harder. He wants to shake you right out of that for which you are believing. But God promises when you remain steadfast in your faith, you shall not be shaken (James 1:2-4)!

Here's a great picture to envision for your life of how to break through the shaking time.

Chuck Yeager was the first man to break the sound barrier in flight. At that time, most people believed the sound barrier could not be penetrated. But each step of the way, God directed Yeager so the day came when he knew it was time to exceed Mach 1, the speed of sound. He had tried before and each time he got near Mach 1, his bullet-shaped aircraft, called the Bell X-1, would shake so much he would lose control of it.

Since then, engineers had made some adjustments but now it was really up to Yeager and the instinct he had for knowing what to do at the moment. And God put those instincts within him just as He has you.

On that day, October 14, 1947, once again Yeager went up in that plane, and as he approached Mach 1, it began to shake and was buffeted from side to side. No one was sure what would happen. It might just explode in midair. But Chuck Yeager knew it was time to break past that barrier. No matter how much he was being shaken, he was going through. So he began to push the plane to increase the speed. All of a sudden, the Mach indicator registered off the scale. Boom! He was through the sound barrier.

What was amazing was that once he passed the barrier, the ship stopped shaking. Everything was still, and flying was as smooth as it could be. It was perfect. Beautiful. He had achieved that for which he had been striving.

When you start to break past the barrier that is keeping you from seeing your desire fulfilled, things will start to shake worse around you. But that just means you're about to get a breakthrough! Yeager's ship was shaking the worst just before he passed the sound barrier. And that's the principle of life, isn't it? You're getting nearer to breaking past the barrier which has kept you from experiencing what you want to see happen in your life—and as you get near, wow, the shaking really starts to increase! If you start looking around at the difficulties and delays and discouragement, you won't go on into Mach 1 with your faith. **Have Mach 1 faith. Push your faith beyond what you ever have.** That is what is going to break you past the barrier. Then boom, you've done it. That's when you'll experience just what Yeager did. Smooth sailing. Perfect. Beautiful.

My Friend, it may be rough right now. Oh yes, the shaking can make it feel as though things are going to break apart, or maybe you feel as though *you're* going to break apart. But remember the shaking gets worse just before you break past the barrier. So even though things around you are shaking, *you* shall not be shaken if you are steadfast in your faith.

The reason the shaking is hard is because you are just about to enter into the place where everything is smooth. You're about to experience the beauty of what God has been doing. You'll feel triumphant. You will have what you were after with your faith. All because you decided you would not be shaken from what God had for you.

A Spiritual Powerline to say out loud:
"I'M BREAKING THROUGH THE BARRIER!"

A powerful prayer to pray:
Lord, this is my time to break past the barrier. So I'm pushing my faith beyond what I ever have by Your power. Now, BOOM, my Mach 1 faith is breaking through the circumstance. From here on out, it's going to be smooth sailing. I receive all that You have for me in the name of Jesus. Amen.

NOTES:

_____

_____

_____

Day 6

Get a New Vision

What do you do when things are not working? You have labored to make something successful or to get an answer to a need, but it's just not getting there. Your goal seems further away.

In fact, you're starting to experience some fallout from it, such as discouragement or fatigue in your body, mind, and emotions. You're beginning to lose the vision you had to see the conditions become better.

That's when it's time to get a new vision! Ask God to show you what He *can* do and *is* doing for you. Allow Him to minister that vision to your soul. It can mean the difference between staying behind with a heavy burden and going forward into the plans God has for you. In fact, it can mean the difference between survival and not surviving.

That's where the Israelites were. They had been in bondage to the Egyptians for hundreds of years, waiting to be set free. Can you imagine how difficult it would be for them to believe their conditions could change? There they were in the mud pits making bricks so they could build cities for Pharaoh. Abused. Many times their children were killed so the race would not proliferate, because the Egyptians were afraid the Hebrews would begin to outnumber them and take over their country.

So these people desperately needed a new vision of what God could do for them in these deplorable conditions. That's when He sent Moses to tell them that they would be freed from their bondage, and God would rescue them with an outstretched arm and by mighty acts of judgment. Plagues would come upon the Egyptians and force them to free the Israelites. Then He gave them the promise of a land where they would go to be free and blessed and prosperous. Sounds great! It was a new vision for them.

But when Moses described all this to the people, they refused to hear him out, and here's the reason why—the scripture says because of their impatience and anguish of spirit and because of their cruel bondage (Exodus 6:9). They couldn't hear words of hope because things were so hard for them. They couldn't believe this was their breakthrough coming. That is the strategy of the devil—to get us "down" in our mind and spirit so that when God comes to us and tries to draw the new vision in our heart, we can't even lift our head to acknowledge the promise of a new place. It just seems too far off.

That's the way it seemed to the Israelites. But then God showed them by His mighty acts of power that His promise was real. They saw one miracle after another as God sent plagues against the Egyptians. Their empty hearts began to fill with hope. Their minds that were dulled by daily drudgery began to brighten. Their tired bodies became pumped with energy. And that new vision began to spring up inside them. They believed they were going to go to the place of promise. That's where God wants to take you—to the point that you can see the new vision and believe the promise of what He has for you, **because that's what will produce the results.**

Don't allow the fact that your vision has not been fulfilled to keep your heart from being filled with hope. Allow God to cause your mind to begin to work on new ways of accomplishing your desires. Oh yes, a new vision is springing up inside you and you will be pumped with so much energy that the conditions won't seem as bad. That's because you know the promise will be fulfilled.

You are getting a new vision of how to receive a breakthrough. God has good things for you. That's in His heart. He wants to see you prosper in every way and be happy and able to work for Him. He sees a content life for you and the ability to overcome challenges.

15

So reach out for all of that today. Believe that you will see this all fulfilled and the answers come to you.

A Spiritual Powerline to say out loud:
"I HAVE A NEW VISION TODAY!"

A powerful prayer to pray:
Lord, I receive a new vision today! I'm asking You to show me what You're doing for my life. I lift up my heart to receive encouragement and strength from You. Yes, I'm gaining new energy to believe for things to be better. Now I will see the results. In the name of Jesus. Amen.

NOTES:

_____

_____

_____

Day 7
_____

God Is Writing on Your Heart

When you're on a journey to see a desire completed, the way can become challenging. Discouragement tries to cause you to cut the journey short. That's when God can help you have the guts and faith to stay with it until you see it completed (Mark 5:36).

There was a scared little boy who was on a journey such as this. His name was Ricky and when he was eight years old his family experienced some very tough times. His father came home and told the family he didn't have a job anymore. Then over the next few months as he began to search for work, he couldn't find any.

So they had to sell their beautiful home and move to his grandmother's house that had been abandoned after she passed away. It was run down and had rats. There were eight children in the family and so good food was scarce. The neighborhood to where they had moved was poor, violent, and inner city, and because Ricky was new and different from many of the other kids, they would bully him and beat him up.

His parents had their own problems. His mother had gone into severe depression and many times didn't leave her bedroom, and although his father had started working finally, it was in construction and he had to work past dark each night. In the midst of all this, when Ricky started going to the neighborhood school for the first time, he was assigned to a fourth grade teacher who was what he described as "soul crushing." Everything she said was negative and unsupportive of the students.

One day this teacher gave the students an assignment and after Ricky had finished it, he did something he had never done. At the top of the paper he wrote the words, "Ricky, the great." He said he doesn't know why he did this because he didn't feel great. In fact, he didn't feel he had much worth. No friends. No one to defend him. But just writing those words, "the great" after his name made him feel good. Ricky didn't realize it then, but that was God's Spirit within him rising up and declaring His truth over him. The Lord was reaching out to this boy to help him know he could overcome the challenges and life could be better.

But the next day when he got his assignment paper back, the teacher had erased the two words, "the great" that Ricky had written by his name and she had written on the paper, "Shame on you." Instead of encouraging this boy during a difficult time, she tried to make him feel as though he should be ashamed.

She may have erased those two words, but she could not erase the courage within his spirit. He rose up in that courage and with faith he went on the journey of life in spite of that teacher. Instead of replaying her words over the years, he responded to God's love and calling inside him. That's when his breakthrough began to come.

The years went by and that boy became a man who finished the journey of fulfilling God's destiny for him. Ricky became a New York Times best-selling author. He said that today if he could speak to that teacher, he would say, "That boy [in your class] was fighting hell every day and, in spite of people like you, he not only survived, he went on to reach millions of people with his words."

In the midst of the challenges you are facing right now, it can be difficult to overcome anxiety or discouragement. **But the devil cannot erase the words God has written in your heart—words of courage and faith.** Yes, you're going to rise up and with tough guts you will face what you have to face and keep going. You won't be stopped from seeing your desire completed. That goal is going to be achieved. There's going to be a breakthrough.

Greatness is coming out of this time. Believe that God will give you what you need in order to do what you have to do to complete the journey to your desire.

A Spiritual Powerline to say out loud:
"I BELIEVE GOD'S WORDS TO ME!"

A powerful prayer to pray:
Lord, sometimes the journey to my desire seems long. But I know You are giving me the faith and courage to complete this journey. I WILL see my miracle answer. You have promised it. And I believe it. Now nothing can take it from me. In the name of Jesus. Amen.

NOTES:

_____

_____

_____

Day 8

Out on a Limb

When you are willing to go out on a limb with your faith, that's when you reach the place where you're ready to experience what God has for you. In spite of how hard it looks, your faith will lift you up and bring you into the fulfillment of the vision of your desire.

But how do you get there? How do you rise above the pain you're feeling today? The bankruptcy that's being faced. A home loss. The child who is having problems. The estranged relationship, or the challenges of responsibility, or sorrowful events that happen.

Those are very real concerns. We deal with all different kinds of things each day. Because of that, it's easy to raise objections of why we aren't able to see the vision of what we desire come to pass. That's why instead of raising objections we must rise above them. No matter how much of a wall is there or how strong the impossibility seems, rather than raising objections, rise above them. That's what causes your vision to take hold and start becoming reality.

You start seeing things from a different perspective instead of clinging to fears or doubts or frustration. You become willing to let God take you out on a limb and teach you to fly with your faith. Then that faith produces His will. It starts taking shape.

One day a family of birds was teaching their young to fly. There were three swallows perched on a dead branch which stretched out over a lake. One of the adult birds got behind the three chicks and started nudging them out toward the end of the branch. It kept pushing until the chick that was on the end fell off. Before it could hit the water a few feet below, its wings started working. It was off on its own. Then the second one did the same and soon was flying away.

But the third chick on the branch was determined not to get off. As its parent kept nudging, it began chirping. You could imagine it raising all kinds of objections. "I never have done this before; really, this is too much. I don't feel adequate! How can I be expected to do something this daring. Above all, what if I fail!"

That chick acted the same way we do sometimes when God is trying to nudge us to fly with our faith. We keep raising the objections. *I can't because of my age. I don't feel well. I don't have favor or acceptance. I've tried and it's not working. I don't have the resources to start.* Just like this bird, we continue to hang on to the branch of objections. But the branch we're on is dead—it's not going to help us get where we want to be. We have to be willing to let go and fly with our faith.

Finally, the adult bird nudged the chick to the very end of the branch, and just as it was losing its grip, it swung downward and tightened its hold again. So how was the parent going to get this child to fly? It began to peck at the small talons that were holding so desperately to a dead branch. When the pain became too much, it let go instead of clinging to its insecurities. Once that grip was released, his wings began to pump, and the swallow did what it was designed to do. It soared.

God has designed you to soar—not hold on to a dead branch. He didn't design you for unhappiness but to have joy and peace. You're a child of His who flies with their faith. You see the Lord do great things. He's designed you to receive blessing and honor. To work for Him and worship. Let go of that branch of objections.

Let your vision soar into what God is about to do. Don't stay with a lower view or expectation. Don't accept less. Reach for something better. You can get it! God has put it there for you.

Go ahead and flap your wings. Catch the wind as it is moving in your life. Be lifted to a greater place (Psalm 103:5).

When you are willing to go out on a limb with your faith, that's when you reach the place where you're ready to experience what

God has for you. In spite of how hard it looks, your faith will lift you up and bring you into the fulfillment of the vision of your desire.

A Spiritual Powerline to say out loud:
"I'M GOING TO FLY WITH MY FAITH!"

A powerful prayer to pray:
Lord, I'm ready to fly with my faith. Help me to let go of the objections. I raise the level of my expectations so I can see what You're doing for me. I will experience all You have prepared. In Jesus' name. Amen.

NOTES:

_____

_____

_____

Day 9

New Get-Up-and-Go

Sometimes we reach a point that we need a resurgence. New get-up-and-go. Then we can feel we're ready to conquer again. We can face new things. No matter how much has been thrown *at* us or *on top* of us, we can push our way through it and up out of it.

It's a feeling in your spirit that causes you to say, "I'm ready." You're revived and surging on.

Now, that kind of vitality and confidence can only come after you have received encouragement from the Lord. Otherwise, too many difficult things oppress you. You feel the stress level going up. There's a challenge in front of you that requires your all and you just don't feel as if you have all to give! Maybe a small percentage, *But don't ask me for 100 percent.*

That's when God can send the right messages into your heart and mind and rejuvenate you. He increases your faith. All of a sudden, you look around and decide that with God's help you can handle this.

I remember when I saw a woman do this so well! She refused to allow setbacks and limitations to determine what she was going to do. When she first started contacting this ministry, she asked for prayer because she was a widow in her fifties and had a desire to be a nurse. Since things seemed to be opening up for her, she felt this was her opportunity to go to school to fulfill that desire. So she prepared for and took the entrance test to go into nursing.

Then over the years as she began taking the classes, she contacted us each time she was about to take a test and we would pray with her, then send her a letter of encouragement from God's Word. She received the encouragement she needed in order to go on and accomplish what God had put in her heart. Two years later, she passed all course work and tests and is now officially a registered nurse at fifty-nine years of age.

How exciting, what get-up-and-go! It was a resurgence in her life. That's what God infuses into you when you come to Him for His encouragement. He wants you to surge ahead in what He has for you. Whether it is believing for that complete healing to come, or that property to sell which has stuck around for a while, or for your business to surge with success or for your marriage to have success. You can feel that your finances or your family life or spiritual growth is needing some help. Ask God for that infusion of His power to come and send reinforcements. You need some backup. And that's what He sends through His Spirit.

Your enemy, the devil, tries to take you off the scene of where you're supposed to be. Take you out of the picture so you can't receive what God has for you and accomplish His will. But he doesn't realize how powerful God's encouragement is. **The Bible** describes it as the type of encouragement and exhortation that's given to urge you on. It is the word used to send soldiers and sailors into battle with courage.

That's what God is doing. He is sending you into battle with courage. He's urging you on, reviving you, telling you that you can go ahead and do this. You can see that change made. That problem solved. Now be revived, as though fresh air is blowing into your spirit. The Holy Spirit is there with you so you can experience revival in your spirit and new determination. A resurgence of your desire and confidence.

When the enemy tries to knock you off the scene, you're going to reappear. You have God's encouragement today and that's going to enable you to surge ahead and experience what He has planned.

A Spiritual Powerline to say out loud:
"I HAVE NEW GET-UP-AND-GO!"

A powerful prayer to pray:
Father, I receive Your encouragement today. I now have a new surge of energy, faith, and courage. My spirit is revived with increased determination to see my desire come to pass. I believe You will accomplish Your plans for me, in the name of Jesus. Amen.

NOTES:

_____

_____

_____

Day 10

Not Intimidated

You belong to God. You are His. That means you are anointed to win in your life. When circumstances are coming against you, remember you're endowed with the Spirit of God and He is mighty and amazing in you!

I know when you're facing difficulties, or you're disappointed because something has not come to pass, it can feel ridiculous to think of yourself as being a mighty anointed person. You look in the mirror and wonder where all that power and wisdom and strength are.

That's precisely how the devil wants you to think of yourself—not as one who can defeat the issues you're facing. He doesn't want you to know it's going to be a cakewalk—a blowout—because those challenges are no match for you. **He's going to try to fake you out.**

This is how one of the most famous coaches in college football faked out an opposing team. Knute Rockne of Notre Dame was preparing to play the USC Trojans, and he knew this opponent was a far better team than his Fighting Irish were. So he devised a plan to intimidate the opposing players.

This was back before the days of eligibility rules, so the coach went all over the town until he handpicked one hundred of the largest men he could find. Each one was at least six foot five and weighed three hundred pounds. Then he put those big men in Fighting Irish football uniforms and marched them onto the field ahead of the real team. As USC players watched those giants line up on the sidelines, they forgot they were the ones, not Notre Dame, who had an undefeated record. They easily could have another win and stay undefeated, but they began mentally preparing themselves for a beating.

Even though none of those large men played during the game, it was their presence on the sidelines that destroyed the concentration of the other team. The trick worked. The Trojan players were intimidated enough that they gave up before the game even started.

Don't mentally prepare for a beating when you are the one who stands in the power and might of God. Don't let the bigness of anything intimidate you. God has given you...

The courage of David.

The wisdom of Solomon.

The strength of Samson.

The favor of Ruth.

You have the faithfulness of Abraham.

The discernment of Deborah the judge.

The excellence of Daniel.

The perseverance of the Apostle Paul.

The willingness of Peter.

Within your spirit is the bravery of Esther.

The vision of Isaiah.

The compassion of the good Samaritan.

The endurance of Job.

The leadership of Moses.

The determination of Joshua and

The power of Jesus Christ!

The enemy cannot win against you. You're undefeatable through the Spirit of God within you. He cannot intimidate you enough to make you stop...when you recognize what is within you.

A Spiritual Powerline to say out loud:
"I AM NOT INTIMIDATED!"

A powerful prayer to pray:
Oh Father, help me remember whose I am and what You have placed within me. I'm not intimidated by needs or disappointment or difficulties. No matter how big they seem, I serve a bigger God. And You have placed power and might within me. Thank You that I am going to win and experience the victory You have prepared for me. In the name of Jesus. Amen.

NOTES:

_____

_____

_____

Day 11

Don't Stay in the Same Place

Fact: we cannot stay where we are and expect to get where we want to be. It's no mind twister. We simply have to continue to move if we're going to get into the place we want to be in an area of our life.

If we refuse to budge in our thoughts or attitudes or in our habits or disciplines, then we'll stay right where we are. If we allow ourselves to become stationary because of our emotions or the conditions we're facing or because something bad has happened, then we won't make any progress. So sometimes when you don't see yourself getting what you need, that may be the time to ask God to show you where to go from here.

I will give you a good example of this in the story of what happened to a Christian man, and you will know him. He has a very famous profile and name. But here are how things started for him. He began a business in 1920 by establishing a ferryboat company on the Ohio River. He got together the funding for it, and the ferry became a success. But he felt he was to keep moving on to what God had for him, so he sold the ferry and started a company manufacturing lamps.

Right after he opened the store, a big company introduced the electric lamp and sold it on credit. His store couldn't compete, so he went out of business. Then he moved to Kentucky and worked as a salesperson in a tire company, but soon that job went away because the manufacturing plant was closed.

The next thing he tried was to run a service station in 1930. Well, you know what happened that year—the Great Depression. So the service station shut down. His next venture was in 1939 when he acquired a hotel in North Carolina, but then it was destroyed by fire and he had to rebuild it.

Now, notice that this man kept moving and going up higher even though difficulties came to him. He didn't just accept what happened and stay in it. But each time that he moved on, he would break through to something better.

So he then started a business of combining a motel, service station, and a café in Kentucky. But just as he became successful, the nearby interstate highway was rerouted. This caused the business to fall off so he had to sell it at a loss. By this time, he was 66 years old. He was on Social Security each month and had a few savings. But he decided he wanted a better position than that.

That's when Colonel Sanders began to cook chicken using the recipe of the eleven herbs and spices that he had from his family. He would visit restaurants to try to get them to offer his chicken on their menus. Sometimes he would have to spend the night in his car moving from restaurant to restaurant, cooking his chicken for the owner and signing them up for franchise rights. Eventually, the restaurants that took his chicken increased their sales so much that other owners began *to come to him* to get franchise rights. In 1964, he sold Kentucky Fried Chicken. Today that business is worth billions.

The only way he was able to experience the fulfillment of what he wanted to do and succeed was because he kept moving. **You can't go up higher if you don't keep moving in spite of the conditions you face.**

You may feel that you're failing at getting the health you want or being at the financial level you desire. Keep moving toward it. Keep moving toward seeing that relationship become better in your marriage, or in your family or with a friend or coworker. Go up higher in expressing your abilities and the talents God has put within you. That thing you've worked on to accomplish—believe it will be so.

There is a day when you will reach a better position in your work or business or ministry. You can see the deepest desires you have for yourself and those who are dear to you come to pass. It's in your heart. You feel it now. Something is not where it should be and you know it. So keep moving.

Refuse to stay where you are because you know God is taking you to a better place. He's put a promise in you and you can obtain it if you keep moving toward it. (Psalm 18:31-33)

A Spiritual Powerline to say out loud:
"I'M MOVING TO SOMETHING BETTER!"

A powerful prayer to pray:
Lord, You know my heart's desires. And I don't want to stay where I am. So help me to keep moving toward the better place that You have for me. I'm going up higher by faith. In the name of Jesus. Amen.

NOTES:

_____

_____

_____

Day 12

Maximize Your Potential

According to Mark 4:20 when you hear the Word of God, those seeds going in you can produce up to 100-fold return in your life. That's when God releases the growth potential of those seeds.

A couple named Julie and Jeff saw this happen in their business. They had pulled up their roots and moved to California to enter into a business opportunity, but when they got there, it did not work out. So financial hard times hit. They had problems paying their rent and car payments; they even had IRS payments they had not made, as well as credit card debt.

Yet, they knew in their hearts they were supposed to start a business. Now that's tough even to think about doing when you're in dire straits such as they were. But when you understand that God can take one seed and release power into it and it will grow, then you can go on. So during this time, God moved on this couple to make a financial commitment to His work. God said that for their situation, that was the seed they needed to give. Now the first thing Jeff thought was, *If I'm struggling to keep my family's needs met, how can I commit what I don't have to God? What am I supposed to do; just write a check out of my income and hope that something happens?* It seemed it was such a sacrifice.

However, after he and his wife prayed about it and discussed it, they knew they had to give a portion to God and make Him priority. The first week that they started giving their seed, Jeff and his brother were trying to get a new carpentry business off the ground. So they went by some construction places and gave the workers there their business information. While they were doing this, they met a builder and he began to talk to them about their company.

Then he asked them if they would be interested in working on a house for which he needed the carpentry work done right away. Not only that, but he was going to do twenty more homes in the next year!

As soon as Jeff got home, he and his wife decided they were going to increase their giving. You see, now they understood the release of growth. The seeds of the finances and the seeds of the efforts which they made by going to that construction site were producing. They were maximizing their potential.

At first, Jeff thought it was a sacrifice but now he says, "As I reflect on the story and what we experienced, I'm still trying to answer one question. What was it that we sacrificed?"

We can ask that for every area of our lives. *How much of a sacrifice is it if I give of my time to grow spiritually? What is the sacrifice if I give my love, forgiveness, or encouragement to others? When I give God priority in my finances or in my plans, how can it be a sacrifice when it's going to result in growth?*

You see, there are so many new things that God can do. When it seems as if there's nowhere else to go, and nothing else can be done as it seemed for Jeff and Julie, God can release something new. He can cause our seeds to grow and produce. So keep putting your seed in. Continue to pray and have faith.

Then get ready for what God is about to do. He wants to release growth into your life. You can maximize your potential!

A Spiritual Powerline to say out loud:
"MY SEED IS GROWING!"

A powerful prayer to pray:
Dear Lord, I believe the seed of Your Word going into my life will produce 100-fold growth. I will fulfill Your plans for me, and my needs will be met. Then others will be touched by You through my life. In Jesus' name. Amen.

NOTES:

_____

_____

_____

Day 13

He Won't Leave You in That Condition

A woman was telling how she had become limited in her abilities because of pain in her knees. She came to the place where she thought, *I'm just getting older.* But God was not satisfied with where she was, and He did not want her to be satisfied. So He dared her to believe for healing. Even though she couldn't see how He could do it, she believed Him. Because of that, she received healing in her knees. When she reflected on what happened she said, "He did not leave me in the condition that I was in. Whereas I was willing to be resigned, He said, 'No, I want you to be healed.'"

Believe God is saying to you, "I won't leave you in that condition. I will change it if you will dare to believe Me. Believe My Word to you will come to pass." Now is a good time to say to the Lord, "I believe You will do this for me." **Show Him that you have faith He can do beyond what you can see.** Remove the limits.

God has filled His Word with stories of how He has done this for people. One of them concerns Moses and the Israelites when they were still marching around the wilderness waiting to go into the place of promise. When you have millions of people doing this, providing food for them is no small matter.

Manna had been raining down each day, but Moses heard the people start crying out for meat. So, he interceded on their behalf and God decided to answer and give them their desire. He told Moses to tell the people to consecrate themselves—clean out their grumbling and complaining and their unbelief and get ready. Tomorrow they were going to eat meat.

Now that sounds great—and it sounds great when God drops in your heart about what He's going to do. But then you take another look at how impossible it seems for things to happen, and you may start thinking the way Moses began to think about it. He couldn't see how it could be done. So he calculated, "Okay, we've got millions of people here. And God has said they're going to have meat for a month to eat. The only way I can figure this can happen is if we kill all of the flocks and herds that we have, or somebody finds a way to gather up all the fish of the sea. That might do it, but that's not realistic." That's. Not. Realistic. Isn't it so easy to begin to think that way?

But God gave Moses the dare. He said in response to him, *Has the Lord's hand (His ability and power) become short (thwarted and inadequate)? You shall see now whether My word shall come to pass for you or not* (Numbers 11:23). And the very next verse says, *So Moses went out and told the people the words of the Lord* (Numbers 11:24). He took the dare. He went out to all those people and announced what was going to happen. Now that takes faith. He had to believe that what was not seen at that moment would become seen by the power of God.

But God created a great wind that spread out in every direction as though the wind was fingers reaching out to grab hold of the quail of the air. And by His power He caused those quail to fly low beside the camp of the Israelites on both sides of it. They were just a few feet off the ground, so the people rose up and all day and all night they caught and gathered these birds.

God had done just what He promised. Moses believed His hand had the ability and power to do this. He believed His hand had not become short, but He could accomplish it. And He believed His

Word shall come to pass. Yes, Moses believed and God fulfilled His Word.

Believe for God to fulfill His Word for you today. He has the power to do what is beyond what you can see. Since He created the universe, He can create your answer. So set your sights on that. Set your sights on what God wants to do for you. Don't believe that He will leave you in that condition. He's coming today to make some changes! He will give you a breakthrough.

A Spiritual Powerline to say out loud:
"GOD WILL NOT LEAVE ME IN THIS CONDITION!"

A powerful prayer to pray:
Dear God, I believe in what You can do for me. So, I have faith that You will not leave me in this condition. I take the dare of faith. Therefore I will have my answer. In the name of Jesus. Amen.

NOTES:

_____

_____

_____

Day 14
_____

It's Just a Toothpick

Here is a mental picture to keep in your mind the rest of your life—because this is how it appears when God is sending something good and important your way. Sometimes when God sends forth His will into your life, the devil tries to stop it. But get this picture—**when the enemy does that, it's as though a toothpick is trying to hold back a flood.**

That's how it is when the force of God begins to move in your behalf. Nothing can stop it. Nothing is going to stop your healing, your joy or peace. No one can bring to an end the progress of that answer or blessing. The fulfillment God has for you will come. And when the devil tries to stop it, his efforts are just the same as a toothpick trying to hold back a flood. All his efforts get washed away, because when God is on the move, He is bursting forth with the flow! And the flow will go! It cannot be stopped.

We saw this happen for a dear woman who is a Partner with this ministry. She decided she was going to believe for the flow of God, so she asked us to be in a faith agreement with her. When she wrote, she made a list of the needs and desires. She didn't hold back anything. That's because she knew God would not hold back anything.

That's really such a great thought to have toward God. **You don't hold back anything when you come to Him in prayer because you believe He won't hold back anything from you.** So when this woman contacted us, she made a complete list. There were several members of her family who were in need of jobs, and also some of them didn't have transportation, so they would need transportation in addition to getting work. She wanted us to believe for all of it. Then she didn't stop there. She wanted her family to have a greater desire to serve God. It was her desire to have them in church and for them to have a good relationship with the Lord.

When we saw the willingness she had to believe for all these things, we stood on God's Word with her for them to be fulfilled. And God began to flow. That's what happens when you pray with faith. God bursts forth with the flow of what you need. He does not hold it back but He releases it in His timing. So God began to go down her list and make miracles happen.

Soon, she wrote back and told us that her cousin had received a job. Then her son got work. After that her brother was made a job offer. Those were answers to the prayer requests for her family members to get jobs, but what about transportation? She continued her letter to say that several of them received cars for their transportation. So now they have jobs and transportation. Next on the list was the spiritual condition of her family to be turned around.

Well, at the same time all this was happening, her brother decided he wanted a deeper walk with God and got baptized. Then the next Sunday at her church, because she had believed for a bunch of her extended family members to show up, it ended up that so many of them came, they filled up two whole pews. For some of them, it was their first time in the church.

What was happening? God was flowing toward her with the answers. And why not? She believed when she prayed and she asked for a prayer of agreement according to His Word in Matthew 18:19. She believed God could not be stopped and that He would burst forth with a flow of miracles.

You know sometimes the devil can try to convince us the flow is stopped. There is no way we'll see this longing come to pass. Too many things have happened. It's too hard. Or we've made mistakes. It's not going to happen. **When all the while that he is talking at us, he's just a toothpick standing in front of the flood of blessing that is about to flow right over him.**

There is a way and there is an answer and it can come to you when you have faith. Nothing will be able to stop it—because your God cannot be stopped! His power and His compassion are too strong toward you. When you reach out to receive them, you can expect results because He will start the flow. And once the flow starts toward you, nothing can stop it.

A Spiritual Powerline to say out loud:
"MY MIRACLE CANNOT BE STOPPED!"

A powerful prayer to pray:
Lord, I believe miracles are flowing to me. And there's nothing the devil can do to stop Your will in my life. Now I receive a flood of

miracles as You knock down the toothpick trying to stop them. I have faith in You. In the name of Jesus. Amen.

NOTES:

_____

_____

_____

Day 15

Something Uncommon Will Happen

It was a normal workday for Peter and his business partners, but they weren't having any success. In spite of how long and hard they fished, their nets were coming up empty in both of their boats. So they had stopped work for the day and were on the shore washing their nets, preparing for the next day, just as when you do your responsibilities and prepare yourself for the next day.

That's when God wants to enter into the common times of life and do something uncommon for you.

This is what He was about to do for Peter and his partners. As they were washing their nets, Jesus came over to Peter and requested the use of his boat so He could sit in it to address the people on the shore. The crowd had gathered to hear His teaching and He needed a platform. So they agreed to do this and rowed the boat far enough away from the shore so Jesus could be heard by all.

After He finished speaking, He turned to Peter and told him to put out into the deep and lower the nets so they could catch a haul of fish. Peter figured Jesus didn't understand, so he began to describe to Him the reality of the way things worked. He had already worked all night and caught nothing in their nets.

That's where we get hung up. When the Lord tries to give us direction to help us in our responsibilities and desires, we begin to describe to Him how things work. *It's just not that easy, Lord. You don't just put your net down and the fish start hitting it. There's such a thing as the reality of life.* But you know, when we allow God to be real to us in the common things, we're going to see the uncommon happen. His reality will become our reality—not limited to our human abilities or resources.

This is what Peter caught onto. So after he had explained to Jesus that it probably would not work, he added something very important. He said, "Nevertheless, on the ground of Your word, I will do this again." (Ref. Luke 5:5.) He and his partners put their nets into the water. A very common thing for guys in the fishing industry to do. But when they did this very common thing, something uncommon happened. They saw a real God come into their everyday need.

He caused fish to come from the North, South, East, and West and hit those nets. Those fish were being propelled by the hand of God. He was blessing these people in their work. They ended up catching such a great number of fish that their nets were at the point of breaking. They were receiving a breakthrough in their business. So they had to signal to the partners in the other boat to come and take hold of the net with them.

I just have to laugh when I read the next sentence in that scripture—because the Lord did not just fill one boat, but when the second boat came over, it says that the fish *filled both the boats, so that they began to sink* (Luke 5:7). It was a great revenue day. God was just showing them how much He cared about their everyday needs. The Lord became real to Peter in his business day. And that's when Peter fell down at the feet of Jesus and called Him, *Lord!*

What had Peter said to Jesus earlier? "Nothing is working, but on the ground of Your word, I will do this." **He was applying the**

reality of God's Word to his common day. Therefore he saw the uncommon happen.

God wants to be real to us as we apply His Word to our lives. We can't just read and memorize Scripture, then not be in touch with the One who causes the Scriptures to come to life. Allow Him to be real in your everyday life—in the common things you do and experience. He will cause uncommon things to happen and change what's common to great blessings and miracles. Yes, God wants to be more real to you every day!

A Spiritual Powerline to say out loud:
"GOD IS DOING UNCOMMON THINGS FOR ME!"

A powerful prayer to pray:
Lord, You know what I'm facing today and how much I need You. So I ask You to be real to me in every way. I refuse to look at the limits around me, but I believe You are doing some uncommon things for me. I'm expecting blessings and miracles and answers. In the name of Jesus. Amen.

NOTES:

_____

_____

_____

Believe You Will Win

One of the things the enemy, the devil, does when you need a breakthrough is to try to convince you that you cannot see victory. He's testing you to see if you will back down and accept staying where you are instead of breaking through to what God has for you. That's why the Lord gives you the ability to face everything with power. Have the confidence that you will win over every circumstance and challenge.

Day 16

He's Picked a Fight He Cannot Win

Have you ever found yourself saying, *I just can't win!* It seems as if every effort you make doesn't get the results you need.

But when that challenge or pain or trouble came into your life it should have made sure it could win before it picked the fight. It's a no-win for the enemy when you call upon your God to move things out of the way and give you victory. Don't worry if the devil is picking a fight with you by sending problems, because he has picked a fight he cannot win. Remember *that* when it seems the victory is far from you. It's not. You have Someone on your side who assures you of victory.

Just think of it in this way. You remember from history how Britain fought many years against Hitler and the Nazis. There was no negotiating peace because they had decided to take over all of Europe and that would be the end to freedom. So Britain did the only thing it could. It fought.

Winston Churchill was the Prime Minister during this time when Britain endured horrible bombings of its cities and much suffering. The country was holding on with everything it had. But it did not seem as if they could win at this rate. He tried to solicit help from President Roosevelt, but the American people were not for going to war.

Then Pearl Harbor changed everything. The enemy flew over Pearl Harbor in 1941 and attacked the aircraft and naval forces of America. However, the enemy should have calculated better and made sure they could win the war before they picked a fight with America. God equipped America with tremendous power and strength of character to face the fight. When Churchill found out that Pearl Harbor had been bombed, he knew America would have no choice but to enter World War II. He now knew they could win the war, so he could rest.

He felt as soon as America entered the war, it was a done deal. They would win. The enemy had picked a fight he could not win. It was just a matter of everyone doing the best they could and staying with it to ensure victory. He believed that much in the power, strength, and endurance of Americans and their resources. The U.S. depended upon God and by His help, the war was won.

We can be just as Churchill was. As soon as the enemy strikes our life, we recognize what's going to happen because God enters the fight. With Him, He has all of His resources and power and strength. Even when it seems we cannot win, because of our God we can say, "We will win!" Victory is ours even when it appears as if there is no victory.

I know as you view your situation right now perhaps it's easy to think that you cannot win over it. There's just too much against you. Instead of saying, "I just can't win," here is something else for you to say in the toughest times—"I have won!" It's past tense. It's a done deal. That's because your God is there, and He will give you victory. The enemies must scatter (Psalm 68).

Britain was facing some of its darkest hours when Churchill could see the hand of God using America to help give victory to the world and ensure that freedom would not be taken by Hitler and the Nazis and other enemies.

Even in your darkest hours, you can rest assured that victory will be yours. You can go around and say from a heart of faith, "I have won!" There is no fight that is too much for God. Keep that in mind when you're facing the surroundings that seem to be so powerful. You're dealing with the power of the One before whom mountains cannot stand. No matter what the surroundings are, they cannot stand still when God brings His power against them. He does that when you stand in faith and believe for Him to give you victory when it seems there is no way.

You may have a fight on your hands, but the enemy has picked a fight he cannot win. As you believe in the ability and power of your God, you can have victory. Nothing can surround you that is more powerful than He. So walk in that confidence and be assured and at peace in your spirit. You know that God will move so you can win.

A Spiritual Powerline to say out loud:
"I HAVE WON!"

A powerful prayer to pray:
Lord, no matter how tough the fight is, I rest in my spirit knowing I will have victory. The enemy has to scatter, because Your power surrounds me. He has picked a fight he cannot win. So...I have won! In the name of Jesus. Amen.

NOTES:

_____

_____

_____

Day 17

This Will Become Your Breakthrough

Believe that a breakthrough is coming for your life's situation. I know that it may seem right now that instead of a breakthrough, *something is trying to break you.* So, here is a truth to remember the rest of your life. **What Satan sends to break you will become your breakthrough!**

I saw this happen in the life of Abbie, my dear sister, in such a powerful way. It all started when I was in my fasting time for that week and felt the Lord speak to me that someone I knew was going to be diagnosed as having a disease. After God's Spirit revealed this to me, the thought came to me that the disease would be cancer. Then as my mind began to race through all the people I knew, I felt there was a certain person this was going to affect.

So of course, right away I went into spiritual warfare for her. I wanted to make sure the enemy went no further and that he knew he was not going to win over her health. Sure enough, a week or two went by and she and her husband called to tell me that she had been diagnosed with cancer. They had received the news that same day, so they were just trying to get over the shock and digest all the information they had been given by the doctors.

I thank God so much that He had given me words of encouragement for them before they had ever called. Isn't it great how God does that? **He prepares our encouragement even before the discouraging thing happens.** And I believe this is what He does many times when our Partners write to us for prayer.

So I described to Abbie and her husband how God had spoken to my spirit about this moment coming and that this illness would turn out to be a step toward her health. Now, that's pretty hard to swallow when you have just heard the word *cancer* and someone is telling you this will be a step towards better health. But God takes what comes to break you and changes it to a breakthrough.

So we had prayer and believed for God's promise to be fulfilled. Even when the enemy sends something against us, that does not stop God from working. He can orchestrate whatever you need to happen so that you have a breakthrough.

The devil was not going to be able to break my sister because we were standing in a prayer of agreement for God's power to break him. And that's what happened through the whole process. She went in for surgery and even though it turned out to be a very long surgery, eventually the doctor came out to speak to the family, and he had some good news. They had been able to complete the surgery and get every trace of cancer. He said she was walking out of the hospital cancer free. What a miracle!

The hospital healing team that helped her afterwards showed her how to walk in better health from here on out. So what has happened? Just what God promised—what is sent against you to break you will become a breakthrough. She is better off than ever.

I think of the scripture that says, *I will rejoice in You and be in high spirits; I will sing praise to Your name, O Most High! When my enemies turned back, they stumbled and perished before You* (Psalm 9: 2, 3).

Remember that your God is awesome and even though circumstances look big, He's already planned for you to overcome them. In fact, He's already made a plan for you to be rewarded with something better because you've had to endure what was sent to cause you problems and harm your life.

So look square at the circumstances you're facing. Do it right now. Just look at them. Then allow God to fill your heart with rejoicing that the breakthrough is coming.

A Spiritual Powerline to say out loud:
"MY BREAKTHROUGH IS COMING!"

A powerful prayer to pray:
Lord, I look square at my circumstances today and I say, "My breakthrough is coming!" What the enemy has sent to break me will become my breakthrough. Your power will break him and what he is doing. So I receive something better in my life now in the name of Jesus. Amen.

NOTES:

_____

_____

_____

Day 18

Ignore the Chatter

During baseball season one of the things we see happen in some of the leagues is the infielders will chatter at the opposing batter to try to get them to strike out. So it's important for the batter to learn to ignore that chatter.

That's what you have to do spiritually when the devil starts his chatter. He makes you think that you're going to strike out. No miracle. No achievement. No hope or help. You have to ignore that and speak out the truth of what God is doing.

When God finds someone who will not be silenced by the enemy and his chatter but will continue speaking what His will is, that's when He can do tremendous things. There's a breakthrough.

David in the Bible had the same challenge. Think how the giant Goliath who was a Philistine wouldn't shut up. He continued to harass the Israeli Army telling them they could never win against him. Every morning he would come out and start his chatter. He had the entire Army of Israel shaking and afraid.

That's when David came on the scene. He was the youngest of his family and so he had stayed home to take care of the sheep. But one day his father told him to take some food to his brothers who were in the army and see how they were doing.

So when David arrived and heard the giant shouting all these things against God's people, he began asking some questions. "Who was this giant to talk to the Armies of God that way? Why doesn't someone do something?" When David's brothers heard what he was saying they tried to shut him up. One of them said, "What are you doing here? Mind your own business. Go back to those sheep and shut up." (Ref. I Samuel 17:28 MSG.)

At this point David did the smartest thing he could have ever done. He ignored his brother. He said, "All I did was ask a question. What is it with you?" And then he went on with what he was saying. **He didn't go back to the sheep, and he didn't shut up.** He knew in his heart that he was there as a destiny from God. That giant Philistine was pushing against the Army of God and David was ready to push back.

He chose stones from a brook and put them in the pocket of his shepherd's pack. In one hand he had one of those stones, and in the other hand he had the sling he had brought with him. Now, what's going to happen next is the same thing that will happen to you as you push back against the enemy and his taunting. He won't shut up, but he will keep coming at you with thoughts of discouragement. *You are not favored or honored; you don't have what it takes. You don't have hope that your needs will be met or that God will take care of this condition.*

That's what the giant was saying to David. He saw this young man who had no sword and just a shepherd's stick and he began to curse him. Then he tried to intimidate him with taunting tactics. He told David he would make roadkill of him and feed him to the buzzards.

Now, David knew this guy was much larger than he was.

He had more strength and power.

His mouth was bigger and he could talk louder.

And his weapons were unequaled.

But there was one thing he didn't have. The name of God. Oh, you have the name of the Lord, therefore you don't have to take what the enemy hands out. You can push back and see God do a mighty miracle.

So David kept talking. He told the giant that even though he had come against him with a sword and spear and an ax, David had something of much greater might. The God of the Angel Armies, the God of Israel's troops. This was *God's* fight and *He* would finish it.

That's when David let go of one of those stones and **with the precision of the Holy Spirit** he put it right in the center of the forehead of the giant. When he did, the giant fell forward, flat on his face, completely defeated.

When you ignore the chatter of the enemy and you push back against what he is saying, and you do it in the name of the Lord, he cannot withstand that. He will be defeated, and just as David and the Israelites, you will have a great victory. So don't allow the enemy to shut you up but keep speaking your words of faith and confidence in God, and He will respond.

A Spiritual Powerline to say out loud:
"I IGNORE THE CHATTER!"

A powerful prayer to pray:
I serve the God of the Angel Armies. Therefore I know I can win this fight. I will not be intimidated by the chatter from the enemy. I ignore it! I hear only the Word of God for my life. Now I believe it comes to pass. In the name of Jesus. Amen.

NOTES:

_____

_____

_____

Day 19

Crack the Whip

It can be easy to become concerned when we don't know how circumstances are going to end up. We don't know what to do about our situation so things seem out of control. What can we do?

Show the circumstances that we're the ones in control with our faith. Here is a picture of what we as believers must do. There was a show that was televising a circus special. In one of the acts, a trainer had several large tigers in a big cage putting them through a routine performance. To make it even more suspenseful, the door was locked behind him. As the spotlights shone into the cage, the TV cameras showed this trainer and the tigers go through their act.

However, after they had been going a while, the spotlights went out. There was a power failure, so there was complete darkness. For about thirty seconds, that trainer was in the cage; it was dark, the cage was locked, and there were three tigers in there with him. Trouble was surrounding him.

To make matters worse, tigers can see in the darkness, but humans cannot. So he was surrounded by huge tigers that could see him, but he could not see them. Then he realized he still had his whip and his chair that he used to control them. So as the production staff was working hard to get the spotlights back on, they could hear the trainer cracking the whip and talking to the tigers. The staff didn't know what was going on, but they could hear him acting as though he still was controlling them. Finally, the lights came back on!

After it was all over, they asked him how it was in that cage when he couldn't see anything. He admitted that at first he did have fear but then he remembered the tigers did not know he could not see them. So he said, "I just kept cracking my whip and talking to them until the spotlights came on. They never knew I could not see them as well as they could see me."

When you feel locked in the cage of the circumstances, and things go dark—you cannot see the future and what's about to happen—fear can try to grip you. But if that trainer had permitted fear to cause him to freeze, those tigers would've known it, and it would have been all over for the trainer. They would have closed in on him. But he was smart. And we have to be smart as believers and know that **even though we cannot see what is going to happen in our situation, we still can crack the whip of faith over the circumstances.**

Keep speaking to those tigers of trouble just as that trainer continued to speak to those tigers he was controlling. Speak against them using the Word of God, and when they try to close in when it's dark, crack the whip of faith. When you do, light flows into the darkness and peace floods into you. Don't allow fear to cause you to run when trouble surrounds you. Face those conditions and let them know who is boss.

When you act with peace, the devil doesn't know that you cannot see the future. All he sees is that you are going around cracking your whip of faith and speaking the Word of God against those circumstances, acting as though you're in control and having total peace. So he figures that you see what's going on. He doesn't have you cornered in a dark cage about to eat up your life.

Then as you keep doing that, this is what happens—the lights come on. Just as they came on for that trainer after he continued to crack his whip against those tigers, so will the light of God come into your situation. The Word of God you're speaking will send light into the situation, and the darkness will be dispelled. Then you'll be standing there victorious! Hallelujah.

You can have peace over fear and conquer it. Those circumstances have to behave. They are not allowed to consume you. Fear of the unknown cannot overpower you. That's when you will experience deliverance and victory. (Ref. John 14:27.)

A Spiritual Powerline to say out loud:
"I'M CRACKING THE WHIP OF FAITH!"

A powerful prayer to pray:
Lord, I know You're with me in the midst of my circumstances. So I have peace. I will not fear the unknown. With faith, I speak the Word of God and take control. I'm cracking the whip of faith. Now light will dispel the darkness. And I am standing in victory. In the name of Jesus. Amen.

NOTES:

_____

_____

_____

Day 20

God Will Support You

God has goodness planned for us as we are willing to yield to His plan. But that means we must surrender to His ways of doing things and that takes trust. We're tempted to try to work it out our way because well...there are times we're just not sure. But when we yield the entire challenge or desire to God, His support is all we need.

This is what the man Moses had to do. He was in a situation where he figured out it was a whole lot better to surrender and let God support him than to try to get out of something himself.

His challenge was managing the Israelites in the wilderness before they went into the land of promise. A man named Korah and his buddies who were leaders among the people had become somewhat heady. So they decided they didn't need Moses telling them what to do and speaking for God to the people. So Korah and 250 men from the assembly came and gave this speech to Moses and his brother, Aaron. *[Enough of you!] You take too much upon yourselves, seeing that all the congregation is holy, every one of them, and the Lord is among them. Why then do you lift yourselves up above the assembly of the Lord?* (Ref. Numbers 16:3.)

They have missed something here. Moses and Aaron did not raise themselves above the other people. God did. Therefore they had His support. When you have acted according to what God wants you to do, then you have His support. He's going to protect you and take care of you.

The Bible describes how when Moses heard their words, he fell on his face on the ground. What he did is very symbolic. He fell on his face to show that God was the only One who could support him. He would strengthen and protect him and help him through this with victory.

So Moses told the congregation of people that they would see who was chosen by God. If those men died a common death, then it was not he who had been chosen, but if God caused a new thing to happen and the earth opened up and swallowed them, then they would know those men had done the wrong thing. As soon as he stopped speaking, the ground under those who had offended God split apart and the earth swallowed them and all their possessions.

When you surrender to God's support and His will, He will cause a new thing to happen in your behalf. The circumstances will be swallowed up by a miracle. He will support you in every way because you have surrendered to Him. **That's because when you're in the place of obedience, you're in the place where miracles can happen.**

John and I both have experienced this in so many ways—where we received God's support because we surrendered to Him. I recall how years ago John was dealing with something very difficult and challenging. So I reminded him how when things come at me this way, many times I get on the floor on my face. That's because God showed me this is a sign of complete surrender to His support as I do things His way in the situation. It really helps. You feel your heart completely yield to God as you lay there on your face.

So right away, John decided to lie down on the carpet facedown, and we began to pray. As I sat there praying, I noticed that John's arms were stretched straight out. So I said to him, "Do you realize that your body is in the symbol of the cross; does that mean anything?" And he replied in his best Charlton Heston-type voice, "My flesh is being crucified." We had a good laugh over that, but it was very true. We have to crucify or nail to the cross our desire to do it our way. It's self surrender. Do you know, because of that, John came out of those circumstances with great victory and growth and saw God's hand and anointing on him.

This is what God has for you as you surrender to His support. Great victory. Growth in Him. Anointing that is evident. You will see His hand upon your life. Believe that He is there for you. You can step out in trust and know that you will be supported. You will be in the place of miracles with God.

A Spiritual Powerline to say out loud:
"I HAVE GOD'S SUPPORT!"

A powerful prayer to pray:
God, I surrender my ways to You today. I rely on You for the answer to my circumstances. Now, I have Your support. Therefore, I have victory! In the name of Jesus. Amen.

NOTES:

_____

_____

_____

Day 21

The Big Dog

Sometimes when we're going through a difficult time, it can be hard not to fear what's going to happen. Or if we have longed for something to happen, and it keeps not happening, it can be easy to fear that it never will. Are you facing something such as that today? You need a breakthrough? Maybe you feel powerless about it.

Remember this: you are tough. So you don't have to fear anything! God made you tougher than anything you have to encounter in life. There is no doubt the devil will throw things at you that will try to make you back away from the wonderful blessings and accomplishments and the healing and satisfaction prepared for you. He'll try to send anything your way to push you away from those so your life is incomplete and you're tormented with fear. But you are tougher than what he can send.

Think of it in this way: a man had some superior hunting dogs. He could take them up in the mountains, and there wasn't anything that was too tough for them to hunt. But there was something funny about these big hunting dogs—they were afraid of chickens.

When the dogs were pups, the previous owner had put them with the chickens. Because the dogs were puppies, the chickens that were much bigger than they were, would chase them all over the place. So you can imagine how those puppies feared the chickens. But now that they were big strong hunting dogs, instead of realizing they were tougher than the chickens, they were still afraid of them.

Listen, you don't have to fear the chickens! You're the big dog! Every time you start to enter into the situation and you feel afraid of what may or may not happen, remind yourself, "I don't fear the chickens." The circumstances may seem stronger than you are right now, but you can overtake them because of the power of God within you. The tormenting size of the conditions is not going to determine your future. The problem is just a chicken. And you are big enough and strong enough in your faith to stand up to it.

You can overcome the hassle at work. When you're sick and tired of a condition remaining the same, say, "I'm tough enough to withstand and win over it." You can win over the discouragement which tries to make you stop working toward the goal you have.

You can triumph over the pain you feel from what someone is doing to you.

When you're tired of looking at unpaid bills or searching for enough funds to do what God has put in your heart to do, you won't fear because God is urging you to arise and see His provision take you into His blessing. You will win over the issues facing you. You'll see the answer come. You'll be standing when the desire is satisfied, because that's how God has made you.

Remember that you're the big dog! So don't be afraid of the chickens—those conditions and circumstances. You're tough enough to win over them in the name of the Lord.

Fear not [there is nothing to fear], for I am with you; do not look around you in terror and be dismayed, for I am your God. I will strengthen and harden you to difficulties, yes, I will help you; yes, I will hold you up and retain you with My [victorious] right hand of rightness and justice. (Isaiah 41:10)

A Spiritual Powerline to say out loud:
"I'M NOT AFRAID; I'M TOUGH!"

A powerful prayer to pray:
Lord, today I do not fear what the enemy has sent my way. I don't fear the future. I arise and go into what You have for me. You cover me with favor, protection, and deliverance. I'm standing tough! In the name of Jesus. Amen.

NOTES:

_____

_____

_____

Day 22

Don't Watch the Waves

How many times have you thought, *Wow, things seem so out of control. They are not going the way I need them to go.* You feel as if you're going down for the last time. You've tried and still conditions don't turn around. Those are times when it's harder to see God when the storm is raging.

We can feel the same way that a dear woman felt who was experiencing this. She wrote to us and said, "Please pray for me; I am going through some difficulties in my job. I know God is going before me, but it is hard to see what He is doing. I trust Him, [but] when we go through the storms of life and we are waiting out the storms, sometimes it's hard to trust until the storm is over."

You know how it is when that storm is so big! It's huge in front of you. If the waves weren't so high...if the circumstances weren't so hard...if you could just see some light in the darkness...then it would not be so hard.

That's the same type of conditions some disciples were facing when they were in a boat crossing the lake. A major storm came up and was swamping the boat. They were so excited that they were in a panic. They were looking at the waves. That's when we get into fear and misery—when we start staring at the waves instead of holding onto the Word.

Now, these men did not just KNOW the Word, they HAD the Word in the boat with them. Jesus was there. John chapter 1 says, *The **Word** (Christ) became **flesh** (human, incarnate) and lived among us* (John 1:14). He's flesh and blood. Right there in their boat. We also have the Son of God, the Word, with us because we have received Jesus. So are we going to look to Him or look to our fears and apprehension?

Will we watch the waves or watch the Word? Will we concentrate on the waves of the storm or rest in what God says in His Word He will do?

If those rugged fishermen would have watched the Word, Jesus, they would have overcome their fears. They would have seen what He was doing and then done the same. He was resting. Jesus was asleep in the boat during the storm. When they saw Him doing that, that should have given them peace that they were not going to sink, and everything would be okay. They would make it to the other side.

But their eyes were filled with the pictures of the waves that were swamping the boat. Peter was probably telling a couple of them to go to the front of the boat to keep it from capsizing. Most of these men had grown up on the sea and knew what to do, but this was beyond them.

You know how it is to be in conditions such as that. It seems beyond you. The waves are too high. But I'll tell you what is higher. The Word of God. When you hold to His Word that you never will be forsaken, then you can rest as Jesus was. That's what He tried to convey to those disciples when they woke Him up.

They woke Him up because they wanted to make sure He knew they were about to sink. *Master, Master, we are perishing* (Luke 8:24). When He saw the storm, He asked them why they were so fearful. "What do You mean, Jesus? Don't You hear the thunder? The sound is deafening. The water is swamping the boat. This hurricane storm is about to take us under. The waves are so powerful." But Jesus knew the Word was more powerful than the waves. So He spoke the Word to the waves and they stopped instantly. There was peace, and everyone made it to the other side.

The Word is more powerful than the waves around you right now. As you hold to God's promise in His Word that you are never forsaken, you can rest assured you will make it to the other side.

What's on the other side? That's where God's purpose and plan are for you. His blessing awaits you. Healing, help, and the answers you need. Your heart's desires being fulfilled. Your breakthrough! It's all there. You can receive it when you push away fear and embrace faith.

Have faith that God's Word is true and when He promises not to forsake you and that you won't sink, you can believe it and you can act on it. Act as a person who's going to make it to the other side and be victorious.

You may still be in the storm, but you're not forsaken in it. You are still floating. Listen, you're going to make it to the very place God has for you. Rest in what He is doing. Don't watch the waves. Watch the Word.

A Spiritual Powerline to say out loud:
"I WILL ARRIVE!"

A powerful prayer to pray:
Lord, right now I have my eyes on You. I refuse to watch the waves, but I am watching the Word. So the storm will be conquered, and I will arrive to the other side. I'm about to receive what I need. In the name of Jesus. Amen.

NOTES:

_____

_____

_____

Day 23

You Don't Have To Take It

Each day when we get up, in spite of what we are facing that day, we can approach the day with authority. The pressures on us cannot make us feel helpless. We are not at the mercy of circumstances. In other words, we don't have to take it. But we can approach things with our spiritual authority!

Luke 9:1 describes how Jesus gave us the power to exercise authority over everything that comes against us and also to achieve the desires God places in our heart. Sometimes I think we see spiritual authority as something we use only to do a religious type of act. But God gave us this so we could do two things—defeat those bad things that come against us so we can experience His goodness, and also to accomplish good things for His kingdom.

So exercising your spiritual authority should be a part of your everyday existence. You should think of it as something inside you that can be used at any moment and for any purpose God has.

This is what a young woman realized. Her name is Jodi and she felt called to do some missions work in the country of Haiti. She had just graduated from high school and knew that she should go to Haiti for one year before she went to college. So she applied and was accepted to help some people in a medical mission there.

But her dad wasn't too sure about this. It was 3000 miles away from home, and the area where she was going was AIDS infested and a very poor country and was controlled by the voodoo religion. But when he talked to Jodi about it, she stood firm that this is what God wanted her to do. So he put her on the plane and didn't know what would happen.

One night she sent an e-mail to her dad describing how she had been called to deliver a baby. Although she had helped someone else deliver one previously, she never had done it by herself.

Here is the picture she describes. When she got to the hut, the woman is on the dirt floor. She's screaming. It's dark. All Jodi has is a flashlight to be able to see. But she proceeds to help the woman. Now if this isn't bad enough, in walks a woman from the voodoo religion. She has on the voodoo garb and begins chanting. Now, would that unnerve you? Would that cause you to wonder about your spiritual authority?

As this woman is chanting, she puts oil on the pregnant woman's head and walks around, then she puts more oil on the woman's stomach. Finally, she goes to the head of the woman, stands there and begins to stare a hole through Jodi.

Well, this baby was just about to come out and Jodi decided right then and there that it was not going to be born with the curse of Satan on it. So she stared right back at the voodoo woman and began to sing with all her might as loud as she could, "OUR GOD IS AN AWESOME GOD, He reigns from heaven above, with wisdom, power, and love, our God is an awesome God."

She said the voodoo woman came apart! She grabbed all her stuff and ran. Then the baby was born with the blessing of God.

Oh, when you recognize your spiritual authority...! Satan will pick up his stuff and run. Instead of his work being done against you and around you, you will see the blessing of God. The Lord wants you to recognize what He's placed within you and given to you to use.

See yourself taking your hand of authority and when a problem pushes against you, with your authority push back against that problem. You have the upper hand, so use that hand to push against the problem and have victory. Whether it's a weight problem or personnel issue or something happening in your marriage or work, with your finances or health—in other words, see your authority permeating every area.

You have what it takes, so you don't have to take it. As you walk and act in that authority, you can see God's great work done in every area where you need it.

A Spiritual Powerline to say out loud:
"I HAVE SPIRITUAL AUTHORITY OVER THIS!"

A powerful prayer to pray:
Lord, I take the spiritual authority You've given me and I use it today. I use it to see Your will done in my life and to defeat what comes against me. I praise You that I'm going to see wonderful and powerful things happen. In the name of Jesus. Amen.

NOTES:

_____

_____

_____

Day 24

Better Is Coming

The picture of your circumstances may seem to be ugly right now. Fear and dread are trying to convince you that things are going to stay that way. The damage has been done. How can things be better?

You may not be able to make sense of what's happening, but refuse fear and dread. Take your hand right now and act as if you're shoving something away from you.

When you refuse fear and dread, your faith can then pull from heaven what God is putting together for you. That will get you through this time so you don't go around upset, hurt in your emotions, and having a problem getting your thoughts together. You know how hard times can do that to us. So you have to set your heart on the better picture God has for you.

I've seen people, in fact I have experienced this myself, who underwent a physical illness or challenge of some kind and they came out better in their health. I've also seen people be plagued with debt and God took them right past the debt. It was gone, and they became more financially sound than they had ever been in their life. This can be true for what you are experiencing. **Conditions can seem to be hard, but they cannot withstand the**

hand of God when you trust His hand. Trust His hand to bring to pass what He has for your life. **Restitution will be given, and His plan, His ultimate plan will be fulfilled.**

This is what the man Job saw happen. You may identify with some of the emotions he had during a difficult time and the ways he perceived what was happening to him. At one time, Job had all his needs met, was respected, and had many friends. He was blessed with a great family of sons and daughters. One day when he was thinking it would be like any other day, his world started to fall to pieces.

One by one messengers came to him to report sudden tragedies that had befallen his household. First his livestock had all been stolen and the servants killed. Then lightning struck all of his sheep and burned them up. The next report was that all the camels had been stolen. Then the final word came that his sons and daughters had all been in the same house when a tornado destroyed the house and everyone who was in it.

His reaction to all of this was to do what was done in that day to signify mourning and grieving. He arose and tore his robe which showed his shock and inner pain, then he shaved his head and fell down upon the ground. Why did he go to the ground? To worship. (Ref. Job 1:20.)

Oh when you've been hit hard and things are falling to pieces, it's time to worship. **You worship while you hurt.** That's what can help you be healed and keep going until God's restitution comes.

There is no doubt Job was hurting as he was on his face worshiping. He knew the source of what had happened was Satan. That's why he described it this way in Job chapter 1. *I was living at ease, but Satan crushed me and broke me apart; yes, he seized me by the neck and dashed me in pieces; then he set me up for his target* (Job 16:12).

Have you ever felt you were the target of Satan and his forces? That's what Job was saying. "Satan has set me up as his target. He came against me and dashed my life in pieces. He broke me apart." Yes, Job felt things had fallen apart. They were in pieces. He was nothing but a target at which Satan could shoot.

But like Job, as you continue to worship God and believe and trust Him, you will rise up from that time of worship and stand with confidence. You will know that restitution is coming. Your God will fulfill His plan for your life. There is nothing the enemy can do to take away what the Lord has for you.

You will see all those pieces that you've watched lay on the ground come together. They're going to form what God is doing for you. Just as He turned around things for Job and restored his fortunes, He can do it for you. Turnaround. Restoration. Those are coming. But that's not all. *Better* is coming. Job received better—twice as much as he had before. He was blessed more in his future than he was in his past. God's wonderful plans were fulfilled in spite of what Satan tried to do.

No matter how small or big your situation is, as you trust God, He can cause His will to happen. Better things are planned ahead. Keep your eyes on that. Watch for the restitution. It's coming.

A Spiritual Powerline to say out loud:
"BETTER IS COMING TO ME!"

A powerful prayer to pray:
Lord, the enemy has tried to use me as target practice. But You are showing me a better picture. Your plan for me will be fulfilled. Better things are coming to me, and I will have full restitution. In the name of Jesus. Amen.

NOTES:

_____

_____

_____

Day 25

Wounded for Me

Jesus provides wholeness and well-being for every part of your life. He became your avenue to healing by what He suffered and overcame through the cross and resurrection.

He was beaten so much that in Isaiah 52 it says that people were appalled to view Him because His appearance was disfigured beyond any human being. He was marred more than anyone ever has been. **From the crown of His head to the soles of His feet He suffered so that you could be healed from the crown of your head to the soles of your feet.**

Why did He endure all of it? He sacrificed to be able to give to you salvation, healing, and blessing. Because He was beaten and disfigured and suffered, you can have victory.

There was a man who came to understand what it meant to have another be wounded for you. He experienced someone doing that for him, and although it doesn't compare with what Jesus did, the story demonstrates what we have received. The man was the Prince of Wales. During the First World War, he decided to visit thirty-six of the soldiers who had been brought to a nearby hospital due to severe wounds.

So he took his escorts with him and the Prince went into the main ward where he shook hands with many of the men. However afterwards, he noted that he had just seen thirty, not thirty-six. So he asked where the others were. The administrators of the ward informed him that the other six were severe cases and in a different section. But the Prince demanded that he be able to see them.

So they took him into another part of the ward and he saw five of these men who were maimed and bruised. After he spoke with them and honored them, he wanted to know why there were only five—where was the sixth man? So then they began to describe to the Prince that he would not want to see the sixth man. His appearance was unbearable because of the wounds he had received. He was marred almost beyond recognition. But the Prince insisted to be taken to him. When he walked in the room, he stood for a moment, then he went over to this disfigured man, stooped down and kissed him on the cheek. As he was moved to tears, all he could say was, "Wounded for me."

As you view Jesus today and all that He endured for you, see yourself looking upon Him and saying, "Wounded for me. Jesus, You were wounded for me." Because of His stripes, you are made whole. And because He did not stay on that cross, but He defeated the enemy and was resurrected, therefore you now have been given the name of Jesus. And by that name, you can be healed in every way.

Envision the Lord standing before you, urging you to take the name that He's given you and all that it represents and all He did in order to provide it for you. He is urging you to use His name to receive and give wholeness and well-being. That's how much power is in that name. It is greater than anything that can afflict you and those you care about—in your body, mind or emotions or spirit. It's powerful because of what Jesus went through and overcame, and now it's yours to use.

He was wounded so your wounds could be healed. What kind of wounds do you have—are they in your body or your spirit? Are they the problems you're enduring in your family or work? Have you been wounded in your emotions or mind? Are you hurting in your finances or overcome by the burdens and heaviness of life?

You have the name and the power behind it to see everything change. You have the name of Jesus. So use it today as you stand in faith to experience the healing God has for you.

A Spiritual Powerline to say out loud:
"I RECEIVE HEALING FOR MY_____!"

A powerful prayer to pray:
Lord, You were wounded for me. Now, because of Your cross and resurrection, the enemy is defeated in my life. So, I receive healing and wholeness in every area. This is just the beginning of what You are about to do for me and those I love. I believe this. In Your name. Amen.

NOTES:

_____

_____

_____

Day 26

And That's That

Have you ever reached the place where you said, "And that's that," meaning the matter is finished—end of discussion! There are times we have to say it by faith.

You may have heard me tell about a terrible time of suffering I experienced for years when certain nerves in my body were firing, which means they were causing terrible pain. I never knew from day to day how bad it was going to be and in which spot it would show up. There were times I would have to go to bed to try to be able to endure what I was experiencing.

In the midst of this, I still had to keep the ministry going and growing—we had just started Alcott Ministries shortly before this.

I didn't know for a while if I was dying or what was happening, but I did know this: I served a healing Jesus. And I had people praying and standing in faith for my healing.

I have to admit to you, there were days that if the Lord had come to take me on to heaven that would have been just fine. Many of us come to that place. It may not be because of physical issues but problems that we're facing. We just get tired of trying to keep going and have faith. And God recognizes there are going to be times such as this, when in our human abilities it's tough to go on. But I tell you from experience, He is always there to strengthen us and help us to believe Him for an answer.

So I continued to believe and ask God to help me. Because of that, my day came. Over a period of time, I saw complete eradication of that pain and suffering. The torment was gone. But the devil didn't give up. As I was recovering, he tried to send a new torment. *This may return on you.* That was the thought he kept trying to give to me. I had to decide, *This will not return, and that's that!*

As I decided to stand my ground and refuse to allow this to take hold of me again, **God gave me the scripture in Nahum 1:9:** *Affliction... shall not rise up the second time*. I grabbed hold of that Word and I've never experienced that affliction again, even though many years have passed. And I never will! The devil cannot use us as a punching bag. He thinks that every time he decides to throw a punch at us, we're there to take more punches. No, that's not what God allows. You may feel like a punching bag sometimes, but stand straight and tall in your faith and say to the trouble, "You're not going to do this again. And that's that. This is not up for discussion!"

You never have to see that financial issue again, that tormenting pain or the constant worry from what's going on in your life. Believe that what's trying to make you miserable in your work or family will be gone and never return. You're not going to agonize over that decision...ever again. That special issue you're facing right now— God will make a full end of it and it will never be able to rise up again. See this happening for what is trying to be taken from you. God will restore it, and it will never be taken again.

And one day—oh yes, one day Jesus will descend from heaven and give a loud cry. There will be the blast of the trumpet of God (I Thessalonians 4:16). On that day, I believe some of the words the Lord will say to all His people and to all the spirit forces are, "Never again! Never again will My people suffer. No more pain or death. No more problems and trouble. Never again will they go through difficulties or humiliation. It's over."

God is bringing resurrection power to you now concerning the situation you're facing. So look in the face of sadness or unhappiness or trouble or regret and say to it, "I'm free and that's that!" Then rejoice at what God is doing!

A Spiritual Powerline to say out loud:
"AND THAT'S THAT!"

A powerful prayer to pray:
Lord, I thank You for Your mighty resurrection power. That same resurrection power within me is overcoming this issue in my life. I serve it notice today that it is gone and never will return. And that's that! You fulfill the promise of Your Word, therefore I am free. I rejoice in what You are doing. In the name of Jesus. Amen

NOTES:

_____

_____

_____

Day 27

Blessed Not Beat

Do you know how God sees your life? He doesn't see you experiencing defeats or setbacks. You were not created by Him to have need or pain. God sees you going through life moving mountains. He put within you the authority to use His power to withstand every challenge and move it out of the way, to have breakthroughs.

The enemy of circumstances will try to stop you from entering into the place of blessing and deliverance and fulfillment. But you know that you don't have to back away. With the power and authority of God within you, the devil can be stopped from taking what is rightfully yours.

You see, the devil is what is known as a picaroon. A picaroon is a thief, a pirate. They are dishonest and cheat to get what they want. Picaroons were especially active during the American Revolution. They would hide in the Chesapeake Bay among some islands that were divided by waterways.

As patriot ships would be trying to make their way to a destination to get supplies to soldiers for the American Revolution, the picaroons would use shallow barges to come out of the reeds to raid the supply ships as they would pass by them. It was greatly hurting the ability of America to get supplies to their soldiers. In fact, it became such a problem that Thomas Jefferson sent a ship which was named the USS Jefferson into that area and ordered it to "sweep the bay clean of this trash."

He was tired of their taking the supply ships and what was rightfully theirs. You see, Jefferson knew he had the authority to send enough power to get rid of the picaroons. Aren't you tired of what the picaroons are doing in your life? You see how the enemy keeps picking off one thing after another? Then remember that just as Thomas Jefferson had the authority to send power to get rid of them, you have the authority of God to send His power to get rid of what's being pirated from you. Stop the stealing! Don't continue to allow it to go on.

Rise up in your authority, then in the name of Jesus send the power of God to stop the pirate. Sweep the area clean of that thief.

Jesus warned us that, *The thief comes only in order to steal and kill and destroy. I came that they may have and enjoy life, and have it in abundance (to the full, till it overflows)* (John 10:10). The devil wants to destroy the blessings God intends for you. He wants to kill the very desire God put in your heart and make you think that it is impossible. He has his hand out all the time grabbing, pulling, and taking from you.

Say today, "Stop that. You are not going to take from me anymore." Then in the name of Jesus and with the full authority He has placed within you, send forth His power to defeat what the enemy is doing against you. He's not going to pick off what is yours anymore. You are going to have what Jesus came to give you. A joyful life. Abundance. Fullness. An over-flowing life. If those are being taken from you, meet the challenge.

The enemy will be beat, and you will be blessed!

A Spiritual Powerline to say out loud:
"I'M BLESSED NOT BEAT!"

A powerful prayer to pray:
Jesus, thank You for coming to give me a life that I can enjoy. You have provided abundance and fullness. So, I refuse to allow the enemy to take those from me. Now, in the power and authority of Your name which You have given to me, I sweep the enemy out of my blessings. The enemy is beat and I am blessed. Amen and amen.

NOTES:

_____

_____

_____

Day 28

Don't Believe the Wrong Message

How many times have your thoughts tried to convince you that there is no hope of seeing circumstances or conditions turn around. The devil is hoping that you will try everything under the sun to find the answer you need, then be discouraged when nothing seems to be working. Your heart's desires are not fulfilled. So you get passively lulled into that acceptance.

But believe that you can meet the devil's threat to you and do it face on. He's not going to harass you anymore. No matter what message he sends to you, you're going to defeat it.

This is what a man had to decide to do when it appeared he had no hope remaining. His name is Bill and he was in a hospital in a serious condition. One day a minister went to visit with him and while he was visiting, Bill's doctor came in. He didn't ask, "How are you doing?" or anything. That doctor just looked point-blank at him and said, "Bill...you're dead! There's no hope. You better get your things in order." The minister said it was that blunt, as though there was no hope. He didn't offer any comfort. Just, "Bill, you're dead!"

What is that? That's the devil sending a threat Bill's way. He's trying to put so much spiritual duress on him that Bill does just that—he believes there's no hope.

After the doctor walked out of that room with that announcement, the minister and Bill just sat there in silence. They were in shock. They had to take in what the doctor had said. Then the minister encouraged Bill to turn it all over to God. And he did. Right there.

Here's what happened the very next day. This is how God can beat what the devil is doing against you when you turn it all over to Him, and you put it in His hands because you trust Him. The day after Bill did this, he was moved to a different hospital. A different doctor came in. This doctor said, "Bill, we're not going to give up yet. We're going to try a different therapy." God combated the devil's answer with His answer.

Remember John 10:10? The devil comes to steal, kill, and destroy. But the rest of that verse tells us what Jesus came to do to combat that. *I came that they may have and enjoy life, and have it in abundance (to the full, till it overflows).* That's wholeness! Every part of your being and every part of your life can be enjoyed. It's full! In fact, it overflows. At times, you may hear the words that your desire is dead. The answer is dead. But wait...new words are coming to you and they are ones filled with life and healing and abundance!

Bill locked onto this truth—and that's really what you have to do. Your faith has to be locked onto that belief just as much as your hands would be gripping onto something if you were about to fall and you were trying to save your life. Because that's what you're doing. **You're grabbing hold of the truth of the Word of God to save your life.** Maybe it's not from a death-causing disease as Bill had, but you want to live the kind of full, abundant, overflowing life that God has for you.

So because Bill had new hope, and his faith was strong, he came through that experience and got better. He was healed. Instead of as the first doctor said, "You're dead," he was ALIVE! Hallelujah!

God is calling you "alive" and whole. Every part of your being—your body, mind, and emotions, your finances and work and relationships, your living conditions and your purpose—everything that is going on in your life God intends it to become whole. You are going to have an abundant life, to the full, overflowing!

A Spiritual Powerline to say out loud:
"MY LIFE IS ABUNDANT!"

A powerful prayer to pray:
Thank You, Lord, that I have been given abundant life. Full! Overflowing! And that's how I'm going to live. I refuse to accept the wrong messages, but I grab hold of the truth of Your Word. I will see Your answers come to me and enjoy life more. In the name of Jesus. Amen.

NOTES:

_____

_____

_____

Day 29

Don't Keep Paying the Bully

If you've ever encountered a bully you know the definition of a bully is a person who browbeats and humiliates another person who is weaker than they are. In so doing, they get what they want.

A man named Jack said that when he was younger, every day a bully who was bigger than he was would force Jack to give him his lunch money. One day he got tired of it and decided to take karate lessons so he could fight back. The training was going okay until he had to pay the karate instructor for the lessons. "So," he says, "I just went back to paying the bully!"

The only problem with that is he didn't realize that eventually the payments to the karate instructor would stop once he defeated the bully. But if he went back to paying the bully, he would have to keep paying him. The devil sends things to browbeat you and convince you that you will have to walk away defeated.

It may seem easier to give into the circumstances, but if you do, you will be paying the bully the rest of your life.

Take faith lessons from the Master. The training will take some time, but as you allow God to teach you how to defeat the circumstances, you will grow. When the bully comes, remember that God has put His Spirit in you, and He is teaching you how to stand up and protect what is yours.

You may be sick and tired of paying the bully of sickness or despair. Debt and need have been taking money out of your pocket for too long. You've watched the bully come into your family or relationship and threaten it. He's tried to work in your job or take over your respect. It seems as though you keep paying the bully every time you look at yourself and you don't see the change you desire.

But oh...he does not know you've been taking lessons from the Master and you're not going to pay the bully anymore. Your faith is growing and you're becoming stronger. Instead of backing away, you go forward in your faith and see God's power do a great work in you and through you! *Get out of my way, bully! You are no more!*

Philippians 1:28: *Do not [for a moment] be frightened or intimidated in anything by your opponents and adversaries, for such [constancy and fearlessness] will be a clear sign (proof and seal) to them of [their impending] destruction, but [a sure token and evidence] of your deliverance and salvation, and that from God.*

73

A Spiritual Powerline to say out loud:
"I WALK AWAY WITH MY VICTORY!"

A powerful prayer to pray:
Thank You, Lord, for making me strong. I refuse to be bullied by what has come against me. I will not walk away defeated. But I walk away with my victory. I'm taking lessons from the Master so my faith is tough. In the name of Jesus. Amen.

NOTES:

_____

_____

_____

Day 30

Shut the Mouths of the Lions

Difficulties, dangers, and disappointment are things that we may have to deal with at times and in many different areas. So we can start feeling vulnerable. That's why I Peter 5:8 warns us to be vigilant and cautious at all times because our enemy, the devil, roams around like a lion. He roars because he's hungry to seize and devour the blessings and plans God has for us. In other words, we have to be aware for our safety.

But this is not an attempt to scare us—because the preceding verse says to cast your care on the Lord, because He cares about you watchfully (v. 7). He's got His eye on you and He's not going to allow the lion that's roaring and roaming to devour you.

You can believe that you're safe in your work. Look to the Lord and not what's happening in your company or in the job you're doing. You're protected from danger. Your finances are safe and sound when you look to God to provide them. Your health is in powerful hands. Your children are in safe hands. You're growing in your relationship with God and He is protecting your relationships with others. Even our nation is safe from threats made against us.

When Daniel was thrown into a den of hungry lions by the king because he *refused to refuse* to worship the one true God, he didn't cower in the corner and spend the night in fear. He was ready when the king came to the den the next morning and cried out, "Daniel, was the God you serve able to deliver you from the lions?" What was Daniel's answer? *My God has sent His angel and has shut the lions' mouths so that they have not hurt me* (Daniel 6:22). No harm was found on him as they took him out. Then the king blessed and prospered Daniel and commanded that no one could speak against his God.

So, when we feel as though we've been thrown to the lions, like Daniel we can believe for God to shut the mouths of the lions. We don't have to cower over in the corner and be worried for our safety. We are not exposed to whatever the devil wants to do, through whomever. But we can still be daring.

I can remember years ago when a person decided to talk against me. They were really making me look bad whether they realized it or not. They didn't understand that they were being used like a lion who goes about roaring. It went from bad to worse. I got so tired of listening to how they tried to discredit me. Even though I believe I handled it professionally and spiritually, their mouth kept going.

So I did what I do whenever something happens like this, I went into concentrated prayer. I continually brought this before God. Then His Spirit gave me the right words to pray. You know the Holy Spirit will do that. When we want God's will and not our own, the Spirit will instruct us of what to say to God so that it's answered.

I believe that's one reason we see so many prayers answered when we are careful to submit and pray according to God's will. So as I was doing this, the Spirit led me to pray that God would shut the mouths of the lions. That sounded real good to me—because I wanted that mouth shut!

So I began confessing this, "Lord, I know You're going to shut the mouths of the lions. They will not be able to continue speaking against me and roaring. I am not the prey because I'm praying." And you know, it wasn't long after that, that this person was completely shut up. They never bothered me like that again. God had shut the mouth of the lion so he could not harm me. Yes, I believe in prayer! I see what God can do.

When the circumstances look the worst, say, "I am safe. God rebukes the devourer for my sake. The mouths of the lions are closed." And you can put other people in that same confession— "My husband, my wife is safe. My children live in safety. My home is surrounded by angels and they bring safety. I have financial well-being. Shelter in my health. Confidence in my mind and spirit. I'm not easy prey. Because I pray, I am safe!"

A Spiritual Powerline to say out loud:
"THE LIONS' MOUTHS ARE SHUT!"

A powerful prayer to pray:
Lord, I thank You that I'm safe in Your hands. You shut the mouths of the lions that are coming against my life and those close to me. You rebuke the devourer for my sake. So I walk in confidence and expect great blessings and miracles. In Jesus' Name. Amen.

NOTES:

_____

_____

_____

Day 31

Ambush

Have you been surprised by a problem recently? Has a disappointment or challenge snuck up on you? You've been ambushed by the enemy!

So what do you do? Do you run? Do you fight? The best thing is to do what the Marines do. Turn on the enemy and take your stance with determination that you will win this. As you take your position of faith and show you believe in God and His power, He will cause the circumstances to be defeated. The enemy thinks he has you on the run, but God will put him on the run. The enemy thinks he has ambushed you, but he doesn't know what an ambush is until he experiences it from God's forces. So take your place and expect that you will not be defeated.

This is the way Marines are trained. This type of thinking is instilled in them when they are being taught how to defeat the enemy. A Marine was describing the training session he went through at infantry school and one of the things that really stuck with him over the years was the ambush training. **He was taught that the best way to deal with being ambushed was to turn and run *into* the attacking enemy.** Now normally when we think of being ambushed, we think of *running away* from what's coming at us. That's our natural impulse.

But what the Marines have discovered is that running away from the enemy empowers him. He thinks he already has the upper hand because he has ambushed you and tried to surprise you by the conditions that he's created in your life. The Marine said when you turn and charge the enemy, it confuses him. It throws off his concentration and ability. In fact, as you rush toward him, it creates fear in him. He begins to think the reason you are not scared and running and you're charging him is because you know something he doesn't know.

That's a picture of what we must do spiritually! Because of the conditions the devil has created, he thinks we will run away from what God has for us. Run from the direction we were going which was God-ordained. Run from the blessing that was about to be released into our life. He wants to prevent us from moving in the right direction, because he knows we will reach the answer, our destination, and the goodness waiting for us.

So we must decide we won't run from his ambush, but we will create our own ambush against him. We're not going to stand for this. So we charge at him with the Word of God. We create power against him by our faith. Wow...that's not what he was expecting us to do. It throws him off. **He sees us rushing him spiritually and he begins to think *we know something he doesn't know*.** So the enemy is thrown into confusion. He wasn't able to knock us off our position. We took our stance of faith, and now he will be knocked away from being able to touch our life anymore.

That's how God wants you to see yourself today. You're **preparing for action** against what the enemy has sent against you. When the fight is over, you're going to be standing in blessing! You'll see victory by the power of God because you took your position of faith.

So as you stand there with courage and belief in your Lord, you're charging the enemy with faith and now he's confused and he's running. Soon you will see how the hand of God has defeated the circumstances against you.

You can face tomorrow because you know God is fighting for you today.

A Spiritual Powerline to say out loud:
"I'M STANDING IN FAITH!"

A powerful prayer to pray:
Lord, today I take a stance of faith. I will not be pushed from my position of victory. By Your power, I charge the enemy with the Word of God and my faith. I believe You are fighting for me, therefore I will see great blessing. In the name of Jesus. Amen.

NOTES:

_____

_____

_____

Day 32

Nothing Can Stop God

Have you heard the hymn, "Got any rivers you think are uncrossable? Got any mountains you can't tunnel through?" The answer to both those questions can be a resounding "yes" at times. You're facing that river; you're facing that mountain. You need some help. I appreciate how the writer of that hymn answered those questions. He wrote, "God specializes in things thought impossible. He can do just what no other can do."

The man who wrote that hymn was facing terminal tuberculosis. This was in the early 1900s and so when you had TB the only recourse was to go to a sanatorium where you most likely would die. His name was Oscar Eliason. His brother contracted this disease also, and as they lay in the sanatorium next to each other, he watched his brother die. Then one of Oscar's own lungs collapsed.

At the same time he felt all his dreams collapsed. He had just completed his education and was ready to start his business.

Now he was facing a river that was uncrossable and a mountain he could not tunnel through. He said he became discouraged and depressed. Things seemed impossible.

But when you face those impossible circumstances, remember there is nothing, absolutely nothing that can stop God. He can take you through the river; He can take you through the mountain.

His power and His love for you are greater than anything you face. It's not impossible.

As Oscar lay suffering in the bed, he remembered that when he was in school, he had met a minister who prayed for the sick and believed God healed them. He also had been reading an article about how people were seeing prayer answered in many different places. God was building his faith to believe for his own deliverance. When God builds our faith, it causes us to let go of the discouragement and start reaching out for what He can do. The impossible!

Oscar contacted this minister, and he came to pray for him. The lung that was collapsed began to heal. He regained his health. Soon, he left that sanatorium and became well. As Oscar Eliason went on to fulfill the dreams God had placed in his heart, he wrote the words, "God specializes in things thought impossible."

When disappointments surround you, things look scary, or there is not much hope, remember God specializes in the impossible. In His mighty hand, He takes what seems as if it never could happen and He makes it possible. See Him taking your need or desire or dream, see Him taking your challenge and what is confronting you, then envision in your spirit His mighty hands transforming those impossible circumstances into the wonderful thing He has for you.

Remember, nothing can stop God when you have faith in Him.

No river.

No mountain.

There is no need or sickness or person or organization.

No difficulty or rejection or legal issue.

Nothing can stop God when you believe He will turn the impossible to possible. Have faith that your answer is coming now.

A Spiritual Powerline to say out loud:
"THIS IS POSSIBLE!"

A powerful prayer to pray:
Father, You see the river I'm facing; You see the mountain before me. It doesn't seem it's possible to get to my desire. But nothing is too hard or too big to stop You. I see You walking before me making the way. You're opening up the path for me to walk into the good things planned for me. I start that journey now by faith. My impossible now becomes possible. In the name of Jesus. Amen.

NOTES:

_____

_____

_____

Day 33

47 Warriors

David Livingstone was a missionary who had a great work in South Africa. But when he first began, it seemed as though it was going to end before he could get going. You know how the enemy comes after us when we've made a decision to do something good in our life—make a change or start something new. But when he sends out his forces, we have a defense against the enemy.

This is what Livingstone experienced one afternoon as he and his group were setting up camp and word came to them that a war tribe had made known they had plans to come into camp and kill everyone that night.

That evening David wrote in his journal, "It is evening. I feel much turmoil and fear...." Now, if he had stopped there, his ministry may have ended there. If we stop with the fear we feel at the moment, that's as far as our desire will get. But he continued writing in his journal, "But Jesus said, 'All power is given unto Me in heaven and earth, and lo, I'm with you always, even unto the ends of the earth'...so that's the end of my fear. I feel quiet and calm now."

When we see the rough or disappointing circumstances, we can say, "BUT JESUS SAID!" We know His power is with us and in us. So when we call on Him in prayer, we're invoking the greatest power to work on our behalf.

That night in Livingstone's camp, nothing stirred. No one attacked them. Years later when he met the chief of this war tribe, he found out that the reason they did not attack was because when they got close to the camp...

They saw 47 warriors surrounding the camp
with swords in their hands.

The Lord had sent mighty heavenly warriors to protect the camp because Livingstone believed in the power he had through Jesus Christ. He also found out that the same night this happened, in Scotland a group of prayer warriors had come together to pray for his protection. 47 of them!

No matter how ominous the circumstances are, when you call on the name of the Lord, He will send the help you need. Warriors are working in your behalf. You can see the tide turn. Victory is yours!

A Spiritual Powerline to say out loud:
"WARRIORS ARE WORKING FOR ME!"

A powerful prayer to pray:
Lord, I have Your power in me and surrounding me. And as I come to You in prayer, You send the heavenly warriors to do battle in my behalf. I'm going to see these circumstances turn around in my favor. Victory is mine! In the name of Jesus. Amen.

NOTES:

_____

_____

_____

Day 34

It's in Your Favor

Do you ever wonder why a miracle isn't happening for you? You're dealing with something in your life or waiting for an answer. You want to see what is on your heart be fulfilled. So you are believing for God to move in your behalf and give you a breakthrough.

But when you come to the place when it just seems that nothing is happening, have faith that there is activity. God is causing a shift. The winds are blowing. Oh yes, there's something going on! God has set it into motion. Knowing this can help your faith stay strong until you see the answer manifested. He sees the struggle and the striving and He's there to help you along. He puts the wind at your back. Blows in your favor.

I'll share with you a wonderful story of how God did this in such a dramatic way. I believe as you hear this, you will understand how easy it is for Him to set the winds of circumstances blowing in your favor. The American forces were fighting in the Gulf War under General Charles Krulak who is a Christian. He tells the story of how in 1991, his troops were preparing an assault on the enemy from the southwest. That was the direction from which they had to come in order to be successful.

The reason this was such a significant concern was because the prevailing winds in the Persian Gulf area blow from northeast to southwest. So if they attacked from the southwest, if the enemy released biological weapons in the air, the chemicals would blow right into their faces. Therefore they had a tremendous concern for this military operation during Desert Storm.

That's when people went into prayer. Not just some of the troops and the General, but the people back home in United States were praying for their protection. The wind had to be changed for the battle. You may be facing a battle at this moment and you need the winds to change in your favor. Believe that prayer and faith can change the direction of the winds of the circumstances.

On February 21, just three hours before the attack was set to happen, the winds shifted from southwest to northeast. A 180-degree change. *This was against the normal direction they blow.* So at 4 a.m. the troops went in and made the attack. As they were fighting this war, for four days the winds continued to blow in the right direction. The winds were blowing in their favor. Then when it came to the point the enemy was ready to surrender, just after that, the winds shifted back. Because there was faith and prayer, God began the work.

You may feel the winds are coming from the enemy and blowing right in your face. I mean they are against you. But just watch—there is about to be a 180-degree turn. Your miracle is in motion. The winds are going to start blowing in your favor. Those circumstances will turn. Instead of blowing against you, you're going to have the wind at your back. There's going to be some divine intervention. Favor is coming your way.

So believe you will see the winds change in your health. Favor is blowing over your business, your ministry, your family. God is causing a miracle to unfold in your relationships and your finances. There are so many issues—and I know some are big and some are not so big, but believe God has a miracle in motion for each one of them.

Believe He is blowing to defeat how the enemy has come against your children. God is going to reveal Himself to you in a greater way as you worship Him and stand in faith. He will do some marvelous wonders in your job.

Feel the winds begin to change! They're blowing in your favor. With them God is sending wisdom and knowledge and resources. You will feel joy and peace and power. The winds are going to blow so much in your favor that it will defeat the enemy—**because on the wings of that wind is a miracle**. And it's blowing right into your life. God has set your miracle into motion.

A Spiritual Powerline to say out loud:
"THE WINDS ARE BLOWING IN MY FAVOR!"

A powerful prayer to pray:
Lord, things certainly seem to be blowing against me. But I believe You are beginning to change the winds right now. They will blow in my favor. The enemy is defeated, and I walk out of this battle with victory. In the name of Jesus. Amen.

NOTES:

_____

_____

_____

Day 35

Showdown

Have you ever wished something was different in your life, but you just kept putting off doing anything about it? Or maybe you tried a few times and you didn't seem to make much progress so it just sort of went to the wayside. Then as time passed, you finally reached the point where you decided, "This is it. It's time to do something about this." That's when something *did* happen. You saw good results.

Whatever prevents you from receiving what God has for you, it's time to have a showdown with it! Have a showdown concerning those things you have worked toward, prayed for, sought God about and not seen the answer or any progress. You are either sick of it or sick about it and it's time to see *something happen*.

What does it mean to have a showdown? It means to face-off with what has been trying to overpower you or someone near you. You rise up on the inside of your spirit and remember that God has made *you* the one who conquers not what is facing you (Romans 8:37). So you decide to confront it and get the better of it with your faith. Sometimes that means you just have to talk to it. Serve it notice that it's not going to get the better of you.

Think of it as a mountain that you're going to conquer. That's what some people decided they would do to Mount Everest. They were going to conquer it. Nowadays, we know that many mountaineers have achieved this and made it to the summit. However, back in 1924 when this team decided to try it with their knowledge and equipment, it was much rougher. No one had ever made it to the top of Mount Everest, the highest mountain on earth. So they were up against the highest and one of the hardest challenges.

Two men from the group moved on ahead to get to the summit, but it appears they never made it because they never returned. Somehow they were overcome by the elements and died. So the rest of the group turned back and went home.

They were from Great Britain and so when they returned they had a meeting in London to describe what had happened on the trip. While they were speaking to a group of people, they had a very large photograph of Mount Everest behind them.

At one point, one of the men turned to the photograph and said, "Everest, we tried to conquer you once, but you overpowered us. We tried to conquer you a second time, but again you were too much for us. But, Everest, I want you to know that we are going to conquer you, for you can't grow any bigger and we can!"

He was having a showdown with the challenge. He could grow stronger and gain more knowledge and become more experienced and determined. But that mountain could not change so they could overtake it. It could not stop them from getting to the place that they could conquer it. In 1953, two men made the first official ascent of Everest and reached the summit. It was conquered.

See what you're facing in just the same way. You can conquer it. You're going to grow stronger. Your faith will increase. God will send more knowledge to use and as you gain it, you will know what to do. Because you've been through a trial, you are more experienced now. You can do what it takes to navigate through the issues.

Yes, you're more determined because you know God will get you to the point that you will see this thing in your life overpowered. So it's time to have a showdown.

Don't allow something to get the best of you, but you get the best of it. Turn and speak to it just as that man spoke to that photograph of Mount Everest. Tell that thing in your life that you're growing bigger. Because of God, your faith and endurance and force are stronger and you're going to be able to conquer it soon.

It's time for a showdown!

A Spiritual Powerline to say out loud:
"I WILL WIN THIS SHOWDOWN!"

A powerful prayer to pray:
Lord, I'm tired of this thing getting the best of me. I don't want to live with it any longer. So I'm having a showdown with my faith. I conquer it by the power You have placed within me. Now I'm going to see victory and happiness in a great and mighty way. In the name of Jesus. Amen.

NOTES:

_____

_____

_____

Day 36

God Is Working Before the Devil Is

When you see the works of the devil against you, remember that God started moving in your favor before the enemy ever got going. All the resources you need to offset what the devil brings against you are available. No need or disappointment can arise for which the Lord has not already devised the answer and the help you need.

You know the scripture in Isaiah 59:19 where it says when the enemy comes in as a flood, the Spirit of the Lord will lift up a standard against him and put him to flight. That means that when something is brought against you, God's power rises up and is unleashed so that it's as an overpowering rushing stream against what the enemy is doing. His breath is a driving force that raises up the standard so the circumstances cannot destroy your life.

You can think of it much like this. A few years ago a tsunami hit India and so many cities and villages suffered losses; it was terrible devastation. But there was one city called Pondicherry, India that made it through with no fatalities. Three hundred thousand people in that city were spared. They withstood this tsunami. Now, why was that? Because 250 years prior to this, France had colonized this city in India. When they did, they built a massive stone seawall. Then year after year, the French continued to strengthen the wall by piling huge boulders along the entire length of it. Five decades later that wall helped sustain the people in that city when the tsunami hit.

When the enemy comes in as a flood, God raises a stronger force against him. But the point is this—it's raised up before the enemy ever sends the problem or need. That wall was built long before the tsunami hit. Remember, God is working before the devil begins working.

You may feel as though a tsunami is in your life, but know that God started sending a standard against it long before it made its way into your life. Believe Him that you're going to be protected. You're not going to be wiped out, left with devastation, in need, helpless, or hopeless.

Your help has already been prepared. You're going to come out of this just fine. Say that to yourself: *I'm going to come out of this just fine.* Can't you feel the power and compassion of God behind those words as you say them? He has so much love for you and has done so much *work* for you behind the scenes. You can't see it, but you can believe it. That's the key right there. **You can't see it but you can believe it.** That's what God wants you to do. Believe that He is working for you now and rest in Him.

A Spiritual Powerline to say out loud:
"GOD IS WORKING FOR ME!"

A powerful prayer to pray:
Oh Father, You see the flood the enemy has brought against me. But I know You started working in my behalf before he ever started working against me. So I rest in You knowing that he is being defeated. You are blowing hard against him. The standard has been raised. I can't see it, but I believe it. So, I'm going to come out of this just fine. In the name of Jesus. Amen.

NOTES:

_____

_____

_____

Day 37

Don't Dance to That Music

Shadrach, Meshach, and Abednego were captive in a foreign land when the King of the land decided to have a golden image made to which everyone would bow down and worship. The signal to bow down on their knees was when the music started playing. But these three Hebrew men worshiped only the one true God.

When the King found out that Shadrach, Meshach, and Abednego would not compromise their faith, he told them they had one more chance before he threw them in the fiery furnace. "Ready, set, and when you hear the music, submit and get down."

Don't you hate it when the devil gives you that kind of ultimatum? "Ready, set, now you dance to my music. Let go of your faith for your family. When you hear my music, you dance to the tune of debt and need. I'm going to make you submit to being dissatisfied. You must live with that bad memory in your heart forever. I'm going to keep playing the music and make you dance to hurt, pain, and depression." Then if we don't, he threatens to throw us into a fiery trial.

Because those three men held onto their no-compromise faith, they were bound and thrown into the fiery furnace. Now, it was time for Jesus to show up! When the King ran to the fire to see their three bodies burnt to a crisp and now submitting to his will, instead he saw them standing, walking free, and there was a fourth one in the fire with them. The Son of God.

You have no-compromise faith. **The only music your spirit is going to dance to is the music of victory that you hear within you.** Expect the fourth Man, the Son of God in you to show up and deliver you through the trial and give you victory by faith.

A Spiritual Powerline to say out loud:
"I DANCE TO VICTORY MUSIC!"

A powerful prayer to pray:
Lord, I know You're with me in the trials of my life. Your power and presence surround me. I refuse to compromise my faith and give up on my desire. I hear the sound of victory music in me. My spirit is dancing with joy because I know You're sending deliverance. I praise You for this. In the name of Jesus. Amen.

NOTES:

_____

_____

_____

Day 38

They're Only Shadows

Corrie ten Boom, a survivor of a Nazi death camp, once said, "Worry does not empty tomorrow of its sorrows; it empties today of its strength."

That's why God's Word tells us not to worry. He knows that it will affect our strength to have faith for His Word to come to pass in our lives. We become fearful and that's all we can see and feel—fear. We don't see the answer, the work that God is doing, the good report waiting for us. The devil has caused us to run from the shadows that he cast across our path. Don't run from that bad picture that is being presented to you. Refuse to allow the shadows to make you run scared.

When you think about it, what is a shadow? It's an image cast by an object which represents its form. So what Satan is doing is throwing a shadow in front of you representing what you dread will happen. He wants to make you fear and worry, because he knows that will take away your strength and peace, then he can rob you of what you desire.

Years ago, God showed me this truth when I was going through some tests in my health. I had been requested to have a CAT scan done and after I did, the technician thought they saw something on the scan that would warrant my seeing a specialist.

So I called the doctor's office and the first thing they did was tell me to have an ultrasound made before I came in because they would need it in order to know what to diagnose and recommend. They said the ultrasound would give them the detail if there was a growth or tumor there.

When the nurse on the phone was instructing me to do this, she also added, "Sometimes what they see on a CT scan may just be shadows. We can't be sure until we do an ultrasound." I realize that this is probably something she tells patients normally. But I knew inside me those words were God speaking to my spirit. I was to believe by faith it would be only shadows and nothing else. I was not to walk around in fear but God instructed me that I was to say to myself over and over every time worry tried to come up within me, "They're only shadows. They are only shadows." As I did that, that truth began to send life into me.

Satan throws up shadows in front of you to try to get you to worry. **Don't fear the shadows.** We see the shadow of the circumstances that are coming toward us and fear tries to take over.

Fear was trying to take over my thoughts and emotions as I was waiting for those ultrasound results. But I was determined I was going to have peace because I knew God would take care of me no matter what. So I kept saying and believing, "They're only shadows."

Then the day before I was to receive the results, I awoke in the night so I decided to go into the kitchen and get some water. As I walked toward the kitchen, it seemed as if every footstep I made tried to say to me that I was going to have bad results on that test. It was the voice of fear giving me those messages. So I stopped in my tracks and I said, "God, You wanted me to believe those are only shadows and that's what I'm going to believe."

Then I turned around to walk back into the bedroom and as I did I noticed the windows where the shades were drawn and as I looked at them I saw shadows cast all the way across those shades. Now I believe God shows us personal things such as that to minister to us. He was showing me those big shadows just to remind me that's all this was—just shadows. And I went to bed. The next day when I got the ultrasound results there was nothing on them that required surgery or anything else.

Don't fear the shadows. And if you do get a bad report, continue to believe it's only a shadow. The power of your God will be there to help you and can turn it around to a miracle. He is still with you through the valley of the shadow of darkness. Though you walk through the deep valley where the shadows are cast across your path, you will fear and dread no evil for God is with you. He's there to protect and to guide you. He comforts you. He prepares a table before you in the presence of your enemies. He anoints your head with oil. Your cup runs over with blessing and deliverance. He refreshes and restores your life! (Ref. Psalm 23:3-5.)

Call those circumstances shadows and know that they will be dealt with by God as you have faith. Shadows must flee because the face of God is standing before them. And they cannot stand before His face.

A Spiritual Powerline to say out loud:
"THEY'RE ONLY SHADOWS!"

A powerful prayer to pray:
Lord, I will not fear the shadows. I know that You are with me and the shadows cannot overtake my life. You're preparing a table of miracles for me right now. My cup runs over with blessing and deliverance. In the name of Jesus. Amen.

NOTES:

_____

_____

_____

Day 39

Make an Airstrike

We can get discouraged when we don't see results to our prayers. However, God wants us to be encouraged that He is working when we pray. Action is happening. Our prayers are producing even though we haven't seen the victory yet.

Here is a picture of what happens through prayer. When an army prepares to go into a territory to get victory, many times the Air Force is sent in before the ground troops go in. They make what's called an airstrike over the enemy territory. That weakens the enemy so that when the ground forces come in, they are able to conquer them and take over.

When you pray, you're making an airstrike. You are sending in God's power to weaken the enemy—those problems or needs or difficulties. Now you're able to defeat the enemy. You come in as the ground force and do your part. That's when you see victory. See how effective your prayers are? They're a spiritual airstrike. There's tremendous power in that.

If it weren't for prayer, America may not have even become a nation. You know the story about George Washington and his troops crossing the Delaware River. They had to cross it in the midst of winter in order to defeat a garrison of enemy soldiers. They won that fight and it was a tremendous victory for the freedom of America. But what you may not know is that it was not meant for Washington to engage in that fight alone.

A volunteer militia group, which had been formed by Benjamin Franklin, received orders to cross the Delaware River and approach Trenton from the South. Washington and his troops were to cross the river and approach Trenton from the North.

The only problem was the volunteer group could not get their artillery across the ice on the river. All they could do was make camp and wait. But there was something else they could do which was much more powerful. The Colonel of this volunteer group ordered his entire army to begin to pray for Washington and his troops who were now on their own to fight.

So they got on their knees and began to pray. What were they doing? Making an airstrike. They didn't have planes or jets or bombs to do it, but they had something more powerful. They were making their airstrike for Washington with prayer and so God's forces were going forth to weaken the enemy. As the ground troops under Washington marched into that enemy camp, prayer had done its work. And they gained victory.

Believe that your prayers are doing the work! You will see action. That's because when you pray, it can make the difference between defeat and victory. When you take that to heart and you believe in the power of it, you'll be very serious about praying and you'll be excited about the results you believe you're going to see (James 5:16).

Every time you pray, you're making an airstrike. You're weakening the enemy. He can't stand up against the power you're sending into those challenges and difficulties. Your airstrike will be effective. Then you, as the ground force, will walk right into the territory and take what is yours. Victory!

A Spiritual Powerline to say out loud:
"I MAKE MY AIRSTRIKE!"

A powerful prayer to pray:
Father, I am making an airstrike right now as I pray. The problem and circumstances are being weakened and defeated. Victory is mine. In the name of Jesus! Amen.

NOTES:

_____

_____

_____

Transfer Your Trust

When you face hard situations, even though you consider the possibilities of what your response to them can be, ultimately, it must come down to the simple but deep truth that your confidence is only in the Lord. You transfer your trust from what you can do to what only God can do and WILL do.

Jeanne Alcott

Day 40

_____

Will You Believe Me?

Once when I was having a very tough time, God spoke something in my spirit that got me through it. It helped me see what happens when we believe in what He will do even in the difficult times.

He simply said to me, "I will help you get through this day. Do you believe this?" Of course my immediate response was, "Yes! I believe." It excited my spirit to think about God caring so much about us that He helps us through each day. But! More difficult issues came, and the exhilaration of the moment when God had spoken was gone. Then in a quiet voice I heard within my spirit again, "Do you believe Me?" All throughout the day, every time it was difficult, there was that question, "Do you believe Me?" Because I chose to believe that He would in fact get me through it, I experienced victory.

God wants to show us how to believe Him in difficult times. **It takes us from limited believing to deeper believing.** That's when we can see all that He wants to do for us.

That's what happened when the Lord took the woman, Martha, deeper in her believing. It produced what she needed. Martha and her siblings, Lazarus and Mary, were Jesus' friends. So when Lazarus became ill, Martha and Mary sent word to Jesus to ask Him to come heal him. But Jesus didn't make it to their town in time, so Lazarus died from the sickness.

When the Lord finally arrived, Martha went out to meet Him and from the first thing she said you could sense how she was disappointed. She said, *If You had been here, my brother would not have died* (John 11:21). But the Lord is going to take her deeper in her believing. It's not too late. She must be willing to

98

believe for Him to help them even though circumstances now seem more difficult than the healing of the sickness. **He can go beyond what her limited believing thinks He can do.**

God wants to pull us out of our limited believing in what we think He will do. When we allow Him to take us into deeper believing, we can see the more difficult issues resolved.

This is what Martha had to do. Go from limited believing to deeper believing. So Jesus gave her the promise, *Your brother shall rise again* (John 11:23). But because she was still in her own way of thinking, she replied that she knew her brother would rise on the resurrection day. Then Jesus said, "You don't understand. I *am* the resurrection and I am life. Whoever believes in Me shall live." Then He asked her this important question, "Do you believe this?"

That's really the question God gives us. **He tells us what He's able to do for us, and then He says, "Do you believe this?" He wants us to go deeper in our believing.**

So then Jesus went over to the tomb where they had put Lazarus, and He commanded them to take away the stone that was covering the mouth of the grave. When Martha protested because her brother had been dead for days, Jesus said, *Did I not tell you and promise you that if you would **believe** and rely on Me, you would see the glory of God* (John 11:40)?

Martha decided to trust Him and so she allowed the people to push back the stone. What is she doing? Letting go of what is holding her to conventional believing. That conventional believing has got to go! It's too limited! So, the stone was rolled away and everyone present saw Jesus call for Lazarus to come out of that tomb and be made whole. And he walked out whole and healed.

If your circumstances seem to be dead and stinking, Jesus is speaking to your heart. You have to be willing to let the stone be moved. Trust Him. Cut with your conventional way of believing and go deeper than that. Allow Him to increase your willingness to believe and therefore receive.

You're going from limited believing to deeper believing so you're going to see the more difficult desires, problems, and challenges taken care of. All day, hear God saying to you, "Will you believe Me?"

A Spiritual Powerline to say out loud:
"I'M GOING DEEPER IN MY FAITH!"

A powerful prayer to pray:
Yes, Lord, I believe You. I believe You will help me make it through this day, and You will take care of the difficult issues. I'm going deeper in my believing, and therefore my victory will be greater. Thank You for being with me. In the name of Jesus. Amen.

NOTES:

_____

_____

_____

Day 41

Sweet Dreams

Perhaps today you're experiencing one of those times when it's hard to keep believing for what you've been praying. What you're facing appears to be a defeat.

You've worked hard on getting this person to respond in the right way to you and nothing is working. You've tried to adhere to the budget and pray the finances in but, hey, those minus signs just keep piling up. Your mind tells you to bail out of trying to solve that issue or get that project off the ground.

But there is just something in your spirit.... **Something deep within you says to stick it out.**

You may feel discouraged when a child takes a wrong turn in their life again. You're tired of all the energy it takes to travel or take care of someone or to listen to that whining kid, or whining adult!

If you were in an airplane, you would want to bail out. But you just can't do it. Faith in what God can do is tooo deep inside you. You believe Him when He says, "It looks like defeat, but victory is there where you can't see it yet." You refuse to see the circumstances as the final picture.

This is what Conrad Hilton was facing when he was first building the Hilton Hotels. Before the tremendous chain of hotels that we see today existed, there was a time when it would have been easy for Conrad Hilton to bail out. Defeat was facing him.

Circumstances had started out great. He began buying hotels, some of which had not been successful with the previous owner, then he turned them around. However, right in the middle of his growth spurt, the stock market crashed and The Great Depression hit. Defeat. That's all he saw. *Give up the dream* were the words that tried to pound inside him.

But his father had taught him to work hard for what he desired, and his mother had taught him faith. **So when he was being forced into bankruptcy, he kept working and didn't let go of his faith.**

He describes how during the stock crash, he kept God's Word going into him. What was he doing? He was keeping the right kind of spiritual thoughts feeding him so his hope would stay alive and he would not get so discouraged that he would abandon the dream.

During this time, he sold the hotels but was retained by the new owners of the chain of hotels as manager. While he was working in this position, one day the turnaround came.

A bellboy in the hotel came up to him and gave him something. It was $300. Now, you've got to understand what that money meant back in the depression. It was big! The bellboy's name was

Eddie Fowler. As he put the money in Conrad's hand, he told him it was "eating money" for him. There's no telling how long Eddie had to save to produce that $300, especially during the darkest days of the depression.

God can send answers from the most unexpected sources. And He sends them during the darkest days when it would be so easy for us to walk away from what we desire.

Conrad took the money, went to Galveston, and eventually got control of the hotels and merged Hilton Hotels with another chain. The rest is history. We know how successful Hilton Hotels have become worldwide.

I often think of when John and I stayed in a DoubleTree Hilton Hotel and the motto was, "Sweet dreams." Hilton had a sweet dream and he did not let go of it. He didn't bail out. But he stuck to it and turned what seemed to be defeat into victory and beyond. And oh, by the way, Eddie Fowler, the bellboy who gave Conrad Hilton $300, he became an owner in the hotel chain.

I tell you, no one can do it as God can. He takes what appears to be a failure or loss and He turns it into a win. **Don't let go of those sweet dreams you have.** I know when you look at what isn't happening, it doesn't seem very sweet. But God is the One who placed it in your heart and He's the One who's going to bring it out and accomplish it. You'll see it flourish. And it really will be sweet. You'll enjoy it and appreciate it.

You'll say to yourself someday, "Thank You, God, that I did not bail out. I kept holding onto this and now I see it fulfilled." (Ref. Romans 8:37.)

A Spiritual Powerline to say out loud:
"MY SWEET DREAMS WILL COME TO PASS!"

A powerful prayer to pray:
Lord, I see the true picture and it's one of triumph. So when I put my head on my pillow tonight, I can have sweet dreams. Good

things are operating on my behalf. I will not bail out, but I will be blessed. I stand in faith. In the name of Jesus. Amen.

NOTES:

_____

_____

_____

Day 42

It's in His Hands

A woman named Michelle was at a hospital with her son because he was undergoing surgery. She had spent the night in his room, and by the next morning, she was exhausted. So she decided to go down to the cafeteria to get some breakfast while her son was resting.

She got on the elevator and when it stopped on a certain floor, she decided to get out there instead of going to the cafeteria. She did this because that floor brought back memories of when she was at that very place years before. She walked over to the very familiar window that looked out over the concrete roof. She had seen it so many times. It was after she had been in a car accident.

After her surgery, the doctors had said that although she would be able to walk, it would not be in a normal way. Also, she would start experiencing arthritis in a year. Then within five years, she would need to have a hip replacement.

But Michelle put this in God's hands. He would have the final say. Now, there she stood, after thirty-five years and none of those things had taken place. She walks normal, has no arthritis, and never had a hip replacement.

As she was remembering all of this and she looked out that hospital window, tears came to her eyes. She knew just as God had her times in His hands back then, He also had her son in His hands. She could be confident in what the Lord was doing.

What is it you are viewing right now? What's dominating your thoughts and your heart? As you think about it, say to yourself, *It's in His hands* (Psalm 31:5). Then be confident no matter what you're seeing or what you've been told, God will have the final say.

We can see this in such an evident way when we hear the story of the man, Lazarus (John 11 and 12). He and his sisters, Mary and Martha, were friends of Jesus'. So when Lazarus became very ill, Mary and Martha sent word to Him to come heal their brother. But by the time Jesus was able to make it to Bethany, Lazarus had died and been in the tomb for four days.

It seemed it was over, but you see, the Lord wasn't finished yet. His timing had to be completed. So when they took Jesus to the tomb with the boulder over the entrance of it, He said, *Take away the stone,* as those around Him protested (John 11:39). Then He prayed and raised His voice with a shout and said, *Lazarus, come out!* Could anything else happen except what He commanded? The body of that man had to come to life. It had to start breathing again. His heart must start pumping again. **Every cell had to respond, because the Word of God had been spoken and the power of it had gone forth.**

When Lazarus walked out of that tomb, he did not appear as a half-dead man or someone who had been in a grave for four days. He came out of there whole and healed. The grave garments were removed and he walked around, in fact I think he probably ran around. **If I were Lazarus I would have gone around shouting, "O death, where is your victory? O death, where is your sting?"** (Ref. I Corinthians 15:55.) Nothing had victory over him. He had been stung by sickness, but it could not have the final say. God's timing was complete and now deliverance came. His times were in the hands of the Lord. So God had the final say.

The Lord comes into your circumstances and He commands the stone that has been rolled over your life to be rolled away. Then He raises His voice and shouts, "Come out!" When He does, everything has to move over. His power and compassion have come on the scene. Nothing can stand in your way.

God is calling out to you now, "Come out! Come out of that trial. Come out of that need, that problem. Come out of that dark place, that depression, out of discouragement. Come out! You are in My hands and I have the final say of what's happening here. It's time for you to see what I have for you."

IT'S HAPPENING!

Things move when God commands them. He has the final say. *O problem, where is your victory? O sickness, where is your sting? Lack, you have no power over me. Complication, you are not too complicated for my God. Difficulty, you're not too difficult for the One who has the final say.*

Your life is under the control of God. Your times are in His hands.

A Spiritual Powerline to say out loud:
"THIS IS IN GOD'S HANDS!"

A powerful prayer to pray:
Lord, I believe You are calling me out of these circumstances now. And You're raising me up. You have the final say over my life. So this is in Your hands. Therefore I have victory. In the name of Jesus. Amen.

NOTES:

_____

_____

_____

Day 43

When You Can't See Far Enough Ahead

It's been said, "Don't be pushed by your problem; be led by your dreams." Refuse to allow the present circumstances to push you into a negative mindset, but allow your dreams to lead you. Be optimistic about the days to come. Believe for good things. Ones which God has planned. You can have anticipation of what He will do.

When you face disappointment or things aren't working out, instead of being ruled by negative thoughts, you immediately turn those thoughts around to think something positive. You're optimistic about what is to come because it's in the hands of God. And He has something better. **Listen to this: you put yourself on a powerful path when you are filled with expectation of God's plan.**

There was a boy who learned this at an early age because of an event that happened to him. Frank was eight years old when his father had promised to take him fishing on Saturday. He was so excited thinking about it throughout the entire week. There had not been any rain for weeks so they felt sure Saturday would be a perfect day. But as soon as Saturday morning came and he got up, he saw that it was raining. It seemed as if it was going to go on all day.

So as he sat and peered out the window at the rain, he didn't feel he had anything to look forward to. That's how it is for us when we are viewing the window of our circumstances and all we see are disappointment and problems. What do we have to look forward to? I'll tell you what—you have God's plan. That's what you can believe is coming, and it will be the best.

Frank was having a hard time with that. So finally he grumbled, "Seems as if the Lord would know that it would have been better to have the rain yesterday than today." Have you ever felt as if you wanted to remind God there could have been a better way to handle a situation, or He could've caused something else to happen to change the way things turned out? That's when it's tough to have a positive outlook.

This is how Frank felt. But his father was just sitting over by the fireplace reading a good book. He didn't have a problem with it, so he explained to his son how the rain is needed so things can grow, and farmers need it for their crops. But Frank kept saying, "It just isn't right." Oh, I have said those words! I have viewed how things were turning out and thought, "This isn't right." It did not seem just. This wasn't the way things were supposed to go. You know what I mean?

But after we have the thought that something didn't turn out the right way, we need to turn that thinking around and start anticipating. Get excited. Because something better is coming. God has a plan.

That's what Frank found out. About midafternoon, the rain stopped. So he and his father grabbed their gear and off they went to go fishing. Because it had just rained, the fish were hungry. So he and his father had a very successful time. In fact, they came home with a full string of big fish.

Then they fried some of those fish, and believe me, I know how good that is. I'll never forget Mother and Dad frying up some black bass that Dad would catch from time to time. It was so good. And so just before Frank began to dive into his supper of fried fish, he prayed with a repentant voice, "Lord, if I sounded grumpy earlier today, it was because I couldn't see far enough ahead."

Sometimes you can't see far enough ahead. It doesn't appear as if you're getting to go fishing when you want. Your desire is not being fulfilled. However, if things happened when you desired it, the fish may not be biting. You would not be successful. God knows when the fish are going to bite and that's when He's going to start things rolling in your life.

Even though you can't see far enough ahead, God can. He knows it all. And He has a good plan. It's something you can look forward to in spite of how the present appears. Believe that the Lord has designed what's ahead for you, and it's filled with the best things for you. Events and experiences and blessings that will help you grow and mature; they will also meet your needs and give you pleasure and delight. You can have fulfillment and greater wisdom and satisfaction. You will be able to help others more as a result.

So change your thinking to be positive and believe for the best to come.

A Spiritual Powerline to say out loud:
"THE BEST IS PLANNED FOR ME!"

A powerful prayer to pray:
Lord, I cannot see what's ahead, but I trust You. I know You have a great plan for my situation. So I have positive thoughts. I anticipate what is ahead of me. And I pull it into my life by my faith. In the name of Jesus. Amen.

NOTES:

_____

_____

_____

Day 44

Jesus Sees Your Faith

Sometimes spiritually we are called upon to see how serious we are about seeing a desire fulfilled. How much do we want to see something happen? Are we ready to tear off the tiles of the roof if that's what it takes? Will we use our faith to break through what is in the way of getting where we want to be?

Think of the four men in the Bible who broke past the obstacles they encountered. Because of it, they received. One day these four men mentioned in Mark chapter 2, heard a rumor that Jesus, the miracle worker, was teaching in a house that was in their area. They knew of a paralyzed man who was helpless to get himself to where Jesus was in order to receive his miracle. So they decided to take the challenge of getting this man made whole. Right away, these four men picked him up on his mat and proceeded to make their way to where Jesus was.

Now, what they did not know was the stubborn difficulties they would face on the way. When they got to the house, so many people had gathered to hear Jesus, there was no more room for them, not even around the door. The people were not going to move aside to allow them to push to the front of the crowd so they could get to Jesus. There was no pushing to the front of the line. Now, some people at that point would give up and take the man back where he was, still paralyzed and hopeless. Maybe try another day.

But these men decided they would not put down the challenge; they were going forward. So when they could not get him to Jesus because of the crowd, they went up on top of the flat roof of the house. There, they scooped out an opening. They tore off the tiles so they could let down the mat with the man on it. As they lowered him, the mat ended up right in front of Jesus. That's what the scripture says. The lame man was right in front of Jesus. So these guys had good aim.

Then of course, the only thing Jesus could do was to stop teaching the Word so He could respond to the faith that was in front of him. And that's what happens with your faith. **Jesus cannot ignore the faith that is in front of Him.** When you take up the challenge in prayer just as these four men did and you say, "I'm going to pray until I receive," Jesus must respond. That's why the Bible says that after they had dug into the roof and lowered this man, Jesus SAW their faith. And when He saw their faith, He forgave the man his sins and told him to rise, take up his mat and walk.

That's just what the man did. He arose at once. His body and spirit responded to the command of the Lord. The one who was weak was now strong and bent down to pick up his own mat—the thing he had been lying on paralyzed for so much time. Now it was no challenge. He picked up his mat and went out before all of them like an Olympic athlete. They stood there with their mouths open and their eyes wide, amazed. They began to say, *We have never seen anything like this before!* (Ref. Mark 5:12.)

And you will never see anything such as what God is going to be doing for you once you take up the challenge. Refuse to allow the stubborn issues to stop you just as those four men did. Tear off the tiles! When Jesus saw their faith, that produced the miracle. No stubborn issue could stop these people but they broke past them. **Did you know that faith can be seen? God sees it. It's visible to Him.**

So determine that you're going to break past all the stubborn difficulties and disappointments that have tried to stop you from going forward. Just as those men, when you find no way to make it happen, tear off the roof so to speak and bring your need right in front of Jesus. Then when He sees your faith in front of Him, He will stop. Respond. And a miracle will be produced. Take up the challenge today and serve notice to the stubborn spirit forces they're going to have to step aside. You're coming for your miracle!

A Spiritual Powerline to say out loud:
"BY FAITH, I'M COMING FOR MY MIRACLE!"

A powerful prayer to pray:
Lord, I refuse to allow stubborn obstacles to stop my miracle. I won't turn away, but I tear off the tiles. As You see my faith, I believe You will release what I need now. In the name of Jesus. Amen.

NOTES:

_____

_____

_____

Day 45

Be All-In

It's interesting how the sports world understands so much about commitment and being all-in. That's because they know victory depends on it. So they give everything they've got and believe in what can happen.

It's the kind of attitude that a successful professional baseball manager expressed once. As he was being interviewed by a radio announcer, the interviewer asked him, "Barring the unforeseen, will your team get the pennant?" The manager's answer was short and sweet, "There ain't gonna be no unforeseen."

There was not going to be any unforeseen because he trusted his team would go all the way. He was all-in with his commitment for victory. Can you imagine if we had that kind of faith in what God would do? That man was one of the most winning baseball managers in history. And that's what we can be—one of the most winning Christians in history if we believe that way. As the baseball manager said, "There ain't gonna be no unforeseen," because our God is in control of what we cannot see. As we trust Him, no matter how things appear along the way, we will come out with victory. But it takes the kind of commitment that says that you trust all the way!

Abraham had that kind of "all-in trust" when he was believing God to fulfill His promise that he and Sarah would have a baby when they were far past the natural age to have one. That's when supernatural age kicked in and they had Isaac. God promised that from their seed would come many descendents and Abraham would be the father of many nations.

Then one day after Isaac was a young man, God came to Abraham and instructed him to take his son and go up to the region of Moriah. There he was to offer him as a burnt offering upon the mountain. Period. That was the end of the communiqué. So what's the next thing that is done? Does Abraham argue with God? Does he break down and cry and go into depression? Does he refuse?

The next verse says Abraham got up early in the morning, got his donkey, his son, and two young men to help him. They split the wood for the offering and began the trip to the place which God had told him. What does this man know how to do? Trust all the way. He is committed to God. He believes the Lord will fulfill His promise that they will have numerous descendents.

Yet, if he sacrifices the only son he has, that's impossible. But Abraham believed there wasn't going to be any unforeseen with God. His team was going to win, and he was going to have the promises fulfilled because he was committed to walking the path God had given him.

As he went up that mountain, he had to trust all the way, with every step. So when they got to the place of sacrifice and the young man asked his father where the lamb was to sacrifice, what was Abraham's response? *God will provide it* (Genesis 22:8). As you go up your mountain of challenges, you have to trust all the way up there. Trust that God will provide.

After the altar was built, Abraham bound his son and put him on it, then stretched forth his hand with the knife to proceed to sacrifice him. This is his test.

So when he got to the ultimate point of faith and obedience, the Lord called out to him once more and said, *Abraham!* Then He told him not to put a hand on that boy. Don't do anything to him. He had passed the test. God was saying, "I know I can trust you now to be the father of many nations."

That's when God's Spirit caused Abraham to see a ram caught in a bush by his horns. He went over, took the ram, and offered it up for the burnt sacrifice instead of his son. So he named that place, "The Lord Will Provide."

If a radio announcer had interviewed Abraham that day and said, "Barring the unforeseen, will your son, Isaac, fulfill God's promise for your descendents?" he could have responded, "There ain't gonna be no unforeseen." It did not matter that he could not see how God was going to resolve this. He just believed in what the Lord would do. **He was all-in with his trust**. That took him into the realm of the miraculous.

Trust God today that there is no unforeseen that He cannot turn around. Committing to trust Him that way will put you in the realm of miracles. Your team will win.

A Spiritual Powerline to say out loud:
"I TRUST ALL THE WAY!"

A powerful prayer to pray:
Lord, I believe You are in control of all things. So I trust You all the way. I'm all-in. Now, I enter into the realm of miracles. I will see my promise fulfilled. In the name of Jesus. Amen.

Jeanne Alcott

NOTES:

_____

_____

_____

Day 46

Is This the Way Things Are Supposed To Be?

As believers we know that our God is the God of miracles. He can do all things. But are we allowing Him to do what He can do? Do we allow Him to be BIG!

Without realizing it, we can make Him smaller and less effective by our apathy to believing. We bring God down in our view, because we come up against disappointment or something seems too big for us. After all, not everything has gone the way we desire, so that may cause us not to ask for so much in our life. **We begin to think maybe this is the way things are supposed to be.**

But God does not want His people thinking less of Him than He is.

Check your thinking. He can do more than you think.

Listen to how the man Job described God when he was having a terrible time and needed a breakthrough. He was standing in faith to be delivered from all his trials and troubles and pains. So much had happened to Job, but even in the midst of it, in verse after verse he describes how big God is, how He does amazing things beyond our understanding.

Then he ends his discourse this way, *Yet these are but [a small part of His doings] the outskirts of His ways or the mere*

114

fringes of His force, the faintest whisper of His voice! Who dares contemplate or who can understand the thunders of His full, magnificent power? (Ref. Job 26:14.)

You're still just on the outskirts of what God can do for you.

You have felt the mere fringe of His force.

Heard the faintest whisper of His voice to you.

Now you're about to experience the thunders of His full magnificent power!

You may not be able to *understand* His power, but you can *believe* it. You can believe that He will use it in your behalf. He can do more than you think. So you need to allow Him to just go to it! It's good to say those words when you're praying and believing for Him to do something. "Just go to it, God. I know You're big enough. And You will do more than I ask. You will show Your full magnificent power! I'm only starting to see what You can do. So I expect MORE!"

That's what Job believed, and because of it, he not only came out of his trials, but he received double of what had been taken from him. He understood that this is not the way things are supposed to be. His trials were not the plans God had for him. He had so much more! So he waited for God to show up and show what He could do. He knew it would be big!

This is what we encourage our Partners to believe when they contact us for prayer. There's one couple who are such dear people to us and we have been praying with them for several needs. Then a few months ago we received a praise report from them, and I love how they wrote it. They numbered 1, 2, 3, right down the list of what God was doing.

Her husband had come out of major surgery and was doing well, getting better and better. A friend's precious baby for whom we had prayed because the baby had heart surgery is now doing very well and they say he is so cute. And some of their family members are doing better in the conditions they were facing. This couple believed their God could do more than what they could see in the natural.

When we believe He can do bigger things, we start seeing Him in a spiritual way instead of with our finite mind. Don't allow the bigness of your trial or desire or challenge to affect your thinking about what God can do. **You can't afford to think from a human perspective—a natural perspective. You have to think from a supernatural one.**

And God gives us the ability to do that by His Holy Spirit within us. Our pea brains cannot come up with the big things He can do, but by the power of the Holy Spirit, our mind is enlightened and our heart is inspired to see the God of miracles.

Believe God can do more for you than you think. He can deliver! Give you a breakthrough. He will cause His will to come to pass as you reach out to see Him as the God of miracles. Don't allow what the enemy has brought against you to be so big in your mind and heart that you cannot sense the bigness of what God is doing for you. This is not the way things are supposed to be. God has more for you. Allow Him to be big enough!

A Spiritual Powerline to say out loud:
"MY GOD IS BIG ENOUGH!"

A powerful prayer to pray:
Okay, God, I'm ready to believe BIG! I've just barely experienced what You can do. So go to it! I want to receive Your plans for me now. I believe I will see Your full magnificent force in action. In the name of Jesus. Amen.

NOTES:

_____

_____

_____

Day 47

Use Your Peace

One of the hardest things we have to deal with in life is the unknown. Those things that are indefinite. We don't know the results of something. We're not sure what's going to happen. Where do we go from here? Everything is unsure and unknown. As we begin to think on it we can get concerned, agitated, and fearful. Then we lose our peace.

But God promises you can have peace when you are facing the unknown! You don't have to be ruled by thoughts of fear or concern. There is no consternation or conflict when you use the peace within you. It overcomes fear and uncertainty and instability. That's how powerful your peace is.

We all have the opportunity to be concerned about the unknown. People can fear the unknown of where a disease is going to go after the diagnosis. Fear of losing their job. Concerned about a court date. Will a relationship turn out to be what they desire? Will a conflict be resolved? What's going to happen in this situation coming up? Not knowing where the next job will come from. And there are hundreds of other examples I can give you.

We can see the unknown as so big and scary! I was thinking of how people lived in fear when much of the world was still unknown and not explored yet. When you look at ancient maps, it's evident how people were apprehensive about the unknown. On these maps, the cartographers indicate where their knowledge of the world ended. Those mapmakers had just so much information that they could map out. Then at the edge of it, because they knew there was more but it was unknown to them, they would write this: "Beyond here, there be dragons."

Sometimes it can seem that way to us. *Beyond what I know, in that unknown that I cannot see, there are dragons. Things that are fearful and bigger than I am. It's something that can do harm to me in some way.* But we have to remember who the dragon is. And it's not the person bothering us! Nor is it the hard thing we're facing. The Bible calls Satan the Dragon (Revelation 20:2). He creates a false picture to us. Those ancient mapmakers had a false picture of the unknown world. Just think if they could have seen the beauty of the world that went beyond what they had seen. They wouldn't think dragons were there; they would know that opportunity, goodness, and wonderful things were waiting for them in that unknown territory.

You're entering into an unknown territory, and it can seem as if "Beyond here, there be dragons." But God is there! He won't allow the dragon to devour you. He will rebuke the devourer for your sake (Malachi 3). So as you face the unknown territory, even if it appears not to be good, remember that God can create a territory that is beautiful, full of opportunity and goodness and wonderful things waiting for you.

So in spite of what you're facing today, in spite of the unknown that's trying to create apprehension, walk in the power of your peace. Be free from the torment that tries to be a part of your life when you don't know how something is going to turn out. You may not know the results, but you know the promises of God.

In His Word, He promises you can live in peace and experience it in spite of what you're facing. That's what you need to remember when Satan is trying to give you a different promise. He tries to promise you failure and problems and conflict. He wants to fill your heart with a promise you won't be taken care of, your desire will not come to pass, the report will be bad. He creates these pictures of nothing but bad coming to pass. Disappointment. Your breakthrough won't come.

He preys on the fact that you are facing the unknown. That's why God made your peace so powerful. He knew it would have to stand up against the power of what Satan would be sending your way. The power of peace is greater than the power of fear, if you will use your peace to overcome the fear. **Don't allow thoughts of the unknown to create greater power than your thoughts of peace.**

Allow the power of your peace to take over and know that God is taking you into the territory where His blessings and help and grace are. Let the power of your peace help get you there.

A Spiritual Powerline to say out loud:
"I HAVE PEACE!"

A powerful prayer to pray:
Lord, I'm facing some things that are unknown. I'm not sure how they're going to turn out. But I'm using the peace You have given me. And it's powerful! So, I overcome this fear and believe for good results. In the name of Jesus. Amen.

NOTES:

_____

_____

_____

Day 48

Wherever You Go

One of the biggest parts of our lives that we must commit to God is the future! You know how thoughts and emotions try to take over. *What is going to happen?*

And that's our mistake. When we allow fear of the *future* to take over, then God who is working in the *present* cannot do as much for us. We keep interfering with our fear. Think about that the next time you sense concern about something in the future. **Your fear of the future can interfere with what God can do for you NOW.**

You have to commit it to Him so He has free reign to work in your life. That's what happens when you hand things over to God. He has complete freedom to do His wonderful will in circumstances.

A woman discovered this in a great way when she faced a very uncertain future. In 1987 she went to a service and as she was leaving the building, she passed out. When she awoke, the doctors attending to her advised that she visit a neurologist. When she did, she found out she had an aneurysm in the major artery of her brain. She was given two choices—she could do nothing and hope for the best or have brain surgery.

When she went home, the first thing she did was to cry to God and express her emotions. After she calmed down, she made the decision to have surgery. As she was waiting over the next few days for the operation, she tried to have faith and thank God for all He had done for her. But soon she felt panic start to take over. You can just imagine when you're waiting for something that serious, it would be a test of your faith to commit your future to God.

And you may be tested right now. You're not facing brain surgery, but you're facing something that is important to you. And you don't know if things will go in your favor or not—if they will turn out the way you desire. A sort of panic can start rising up within you.

So this woman was having anything but peace. She started experiencing all the effects of worry which most of us have felt, such as not being able to rest at night, talking for hours on end with her spouse about it. But it was still so weird to believe it was happening to her. Have you ever had that feeling? *I can't believe it's happening to me.*

So she decided to a find way to keep her mind centered on God and what He was doing for her future and what it would mean for the rest of her life. So one night when she couldn't rest, she picked up her Bible and was directed to Joshua 1:9 which says, *Be strong and courageous. Do not be terrified; do not be discouraged, for the Lord Your God will be with you wherever you go.*

So she tore a piece of paper from her notepad and copied the verse down, then held it in her hand. When she did, the fear of the future drained away. See what's happening? **Fear was being drained of its power over her and now the power of faith could take over.** Fear could not interfere with her future.

So she continued to have that piece of paper with her every day, even up to the time when they were taking her into the operating room. When one of the nurses found the piece of paper in her hand, she said, "I have to take it now; but when you wake up, you will find it taped to your hand."

Twenty-six hours after surgery and recovery, the woman woke up to see the nurse smiling at her. When she opened her fist, there taped to her hand was that scripture. *For the Lord your God will be with you wherever you go.* He continued to be with her over the days, weeks, and months of recovery. Fear had been defeated and peace had made the way for her miracle.

Make the way for your miracle. Commit to God what you're experiencing and that will take away fear of the future and give Him full reign to do great work.

Tape a scripture to your hand or just put it somewhere you can see it often—do whatever you have to keep the Word in front of you so that fear will be drained of its power and the power of peace will enter into you. Your future will be committed to God, and oh when God has it, He can do so much good for you.

A Spiritual Powerline to say out loud:
"GOD HAS MY FUTURE!"

A powerful prayer to pray:
Lord, I believe my future is in Your hands. Therefore I will not allow fear to interfere. I trust that You will make sure that I'm taken care of. I will see my desire fulfilled by Your power. In the name of Jesus. Amen.

Jeanne Alcott

NOTES:

_____

_____

_____

Day 49

What Is Your Echo

The words that you speak become an echo in your life. When you send out God's Word from your heart and mouth, those words come back to you and can produce God's power and His will.

The problem is every day there are opposing words, thoughts, and ideas being thrown at you. It can be hard not to echo those words and have them come back into you. When that happens, they weaken and sap your strength, because they are opposing what God has for you.

A boy discovered the reality of this truth at an early age and it saved his life when he became older. Louis Mayer got into a fight at school with another boy and afterwards he was so mad that he decided he would get revenge somehow. As he was going home he was talking to himself about what he would do to the other boy if he ever got the chance. There were some friends with him who were encouraging him in this, so eventually it escalated to the point that Louis began to curse the other boy with his words. Although Louis' mother overheard this, she decided not to say anything at that time.

The next day the whole family went for a picnic near the mountains where they lived in Canada. After a while, his mother called him over to her and said, "Come here a moment. I want to show you something." She took Louis to an area that was facing a big mountain that almost completely surrounded them. Then she said, "Now, Louis, say the words I heard you say yesterday."

So Louis repeated the words very quietly. His mother told him, "Son, whatever you say, you must be willing to say it as loud as you can. Shout it for all to hear." Even though he did not want to do it, because his mother insisted, he shouted out those bad words as loud as he could. When he did, they echoed off the mountain and came right back to him. It was as if the strength of those words which cursed instead of blessed were coming against *him*. It was a terrible feeling.

Then his mother said, "Now, try it another way. Say, 'Bless you!'" The boy took a deep breath and shouted with all his might, "Bless you!" The echo of those good strong words came back to him. "Bless you!" Then his mother asked him, "Which do you prefer, son? It's up to you. **Your life creates an echo.** Every day, every hour, you have that choice."

He remembered that for the rest of his life. As the years went by and Louis grew up, he was in a terrible accident which almost killed him. The doctors didn't know if he was going to pull out of it. As he was in the hospital in pain, he remembered the echo experience. So he said to himself, "I'm not afraid to die, but I want to live." As soon as he said the word "live" it became an echo which came back to him. LIVE!

He knew that was from God so he continued to say it over and over. It came alive and worked within him. Soon he regained his strength and recovered! The echo of blessing had come back into him and God was able to use the life of those words to give him health.

What's your echo? Blessing instead of cursing? Thankfulness instead of complaining? Victory instead of defeat?

When you speak the Word of God, it is *effectually at work in you who believe [exercising its superhuman power in those who adhere to and trust in and rely on it]* (I Thessalonians 2:13).

I encourage you especially this week to say words such as, "Victory! Healing! Direction!" Say whatever you need, then allow the echo to come into you and give you what you are speaking out. Those words guard and keep you. They set your future to be a good one. You'll be strong and able. Make your echo one of blessing!

A Spiritual Powerline to say out loud:
"BLESS YOU!"

A powerful prayer to pray:
Lord, right now I speak Your words that I want to echo into my life. As I say them I believe I will feel the life of those words begin to be activated in me. So I speak out, "Blessing! Health! Provision! Solutions! Breakthrough! Love, peace, joy!" (Now, I encourage you to add what words God's Spirit is bringing to your mind that you need to say for your life.) In the name of Jesus. Amen.

NOTES:

_____

_____

_____

Day 50
_____

The Miracle Baby

Jesus' life on earth began with a miracle. Then as a Man, He did tremendous miracles during His ministry. And He is doing tremendous works still. But to receive those for your own life, you not only must believe in miracles, but also believe THEY ARE FOR YOU!

That's where faith is challenged.

That's because our enemy, the devil, has done everything he can to diminish the possibilities of miracles happening for you. He tries to make you believe they were for the past, or they are for certain people only, or everything has to be just right for you to receive one. Have perfect faith. Perfect living. And the lies go on.

But God's Word says that just as Jesus did miracles for imperfect people thousands of years ago, He will do them for us today. He is the same yesterday—and not only yesterday, but today, right now in this moment of your existence. And He will be the same forever (Hebrews 13:8). That means He did miracles in the past when He was here on earth, He does miracles now, and He always will. He's always giving them to us if we will believe and receive. Oh what we miss when we don't reach out for a miracle—for big things and in everyday ways.

One day we received a letter from a friend and Partner who contacted us to join in prayer for her baby nephew that had just been born. They discovered that he had fluid in his lungs and was under observation in the neonatal ICU. Now, that's when you better believe in a miracle.

On the same day we received the message to pray for this baby, something unusual happened. I had just finished working on a teaching in which I was talking about *birthing a big baby.* I was referring to birthing our big dreams and seeing them grow. Then all of a sudden I received this request to pray for a baby who had been born and was struggling to live.

So I asked John to pass on to the family that I had just been teaching on birthing a BIG baby at the same time I had received the prayer request. That meant so much to them because this baby was in fact big—over nine pounds. Now isn't God amazing and amusing at times. What better way could He speak to this family that He was aware of what was happening?

Sometime later we received a letter saying that even though it was a trying time for the family, God came through for them and this wonderful big baby was discharged from the ICU six days after

125

he was born and allowed to go home. They are calling him their miracle baby!

Thank goodness we believe in miracles, and even beyond that, we believe they are for us. Would anyone want to hold that baby in their arms and say, "I'm so sorry, little one, but miracles don't happen anymore. Jesus is not the same today so He doesn't do miracles now. He simply can't help you." We would never think of doing that. Yet, as we go throughout each day, are we accepting that lie to us?

The Lord wants you to receive miracles from His hand. That's what He communicated to you when a miracle Baby was born thousands of years ago who became the Messiah of Miracles. Because of Him, you not only can have eternal redemption, but you can receive miracles for every area of your life.

Today feel the touch of the Messiah—the miracle touch. He's touching your heart so you are ready to believe and receive.

A Spiritual Powerline to say out loud:
"I RECEIVE MY MIRACLE!"

A powerful prayer to pray:
Lord, I believe miracles are for me. You've already planned them and prepared them. So today by my faith, I receive my miracles. Life is going to be different! I will see supernatural things happen beginning soon. I praise You for it. In the name of Jesus. Amen.

NOTES:

_____

_____

_____

Day 51

Mercies for What You Need

Have you ever gone around singing that wonderful hymn, "Morning by morning new mercies I see. All I have needed Your hand has provided"? The name of the hymn is, "Great Is Thy Faithfulness" and it is played by Daniel Kleefeld on our broadcast each day.

Thomas Chisholm is the person who wrote that song and there was a reason he could say, "Morning by morning new mercies I see." It was because there were years when he didn't have good health and it affected his income. He went through years of financial struggle and each day had to believe for enough funds. However, one day he was thinking of how in spite of his income, God had always given him the assistance he must have. Every day when he woke up, what he must have in order for his needs to be met showed up.

He was so thankful for this that he said, "[God] has given me many wonderful displays of His providing care which have filled me with astonishing gratefulness." Then he penned those words, "Great is Thy faithfulness! Morning by morning new mercies I see. All I have needed Your hand has provided."

Lamentations chapter 3 says that God's mercies are **created new every morning** (MSG). The writer of that scripture had experienced hard times, but when he thought about the mercies that were there to help him through it all, he said that in spite of hardships, **Yet I still dare to hope when I remember this** (Lamentations 3:21 NLT). He was saying, "When I remember that God's mercies are new every morning, I dare to hope for all I need."

That's why we need to be sure we remember each day that God has created new mercies for us. Otherwise the hope can get sucked right out of us when we see what isn't going right, we feel the pain, or see our desire that isn't being fulfilled, the problem that faces us, the fear we have. Remember during those times, you have God's divine favor and blessing and you will see the evidence of them when you hope. You still dare to hope because you remember He's created new mercies for you to handle what's going on that day.

Just imagine God watching over you as you wake up each morning. He sees you starting to get out of bed and so He says, "It's time. I must release on them the new mercies that I created this morning especially for them. I'm sending My divine favor to help them in every situation." Now that makes getting up in the morning much easier. You can envision those mercies coming into your life—they go before you and surround you. They create the path for you to walk.

So if you stumble in that path or you hit a bad spot in the day, **reach out and grab for your mercies from God**. Just reach out with your faith and say, "Lord! I need the mercies You've created for me. I need them now." Then tell Him you want them to go into effect and help you.

That's one of the blessings that new mercies give you every day—they are there to give you assistance! Everywhere you go and everything you do, mercies have been created to help you and assist you that day.

Every day you get up, you are not walking by yourself. Every step you take, all that you have to do or face, God's hand is there to provide all you need. **Believe you will see the evidence of His mercies that have been created just for you that day—grab them with your faith. Morning by morning new mercies you will see.**

A Spiritual Powerline to say out loud:
"I HAVE NEW MERCIES ON ME TODAY!"

A powerful prayer to pray:
Thank You, Lord, that You are there to provide all I need. I ask
You to pour on me the new mercies You have created for today. I
still dare to hope because of Your mercies—Your divine favor and
blessing on my life. I know I will see a great breakthrough. In the
name of Jesus. Amen.

NOTES:

_____

_____

_____

Day 52

God Has a Gift for You

Refuse to allow the problems of the day to cause you to miss what God is doing. He's working some things together for you. When it seems as though it's the end, it can be the beginning.

A minister, Steve, was going through a hard time and came to the point that he told his wife, "I'm quitting the ministry. And this time I mean it." You know how we can threaten to quit something, and then we feel in order to make sure everybody knows we are serious about it, we add, "And this time I mean it." That's where Steve was.

His wife recognized he was going through a tough time and needed to have his heart renewed and his mind cleared, so she suggested that he go for a drive and think things through. Then she added, "While you're out, would you be a sweetheart and pick me up a burrito?" It was obvious that she wasn't too worried because she knew he would make it through this time and that God would show him what He was doing in his life.

So Steve got in the car, drove around for an hour, complained to God, and then decided to get the burrito for his wife. As he was in the drive-through, he sensed God's Spirit give him an impression that if he would open the car door, He was going to give him a gift. That seemed odd, but it was such a strong impression that he opened the door of his car and looked down. There was a penny smashed into the road. He pried the penny out of the asphalt and closed his door.

He thought it wasn't much of a gift, until God gave him this word: "Many people in the city feel about as valuable as discarded pennies. I'm giving you the gift of gathering people who seem to have no value. Though these are the people that the world casts off, they have great value to Me. If you open your heart, I will send you more *pennies* than you know what to do with."

Steve did open his heart and pushed discouragement out of it. Then he took courage and received the gift God was giving him. He and his wife now have a church that brings in people who don't feel they have value, and they minister to them. It has grown into an attendance of thousands and great things are happening through it in the community. He sees how God was working things together for a breakthrough. It wasn't the end even though he felt that he wanted to quit. It was actually the beginning.

On tough days, when things are not going well, get excited about the gift that God is working on for you. He's putting something together that will change the circumstances. He knows how to fulfill you and take care of your needs and bring you to the place He has for your life. Trust Him with that and open up your heart. Push discouragement out of it (Numbers 32:9). Then receive the excitement God wants you to feel because of the gift you are about to receive.

A Spiritual Powerline to say out loud:
"I'M ABOUT TO RECEIVE A GIFT!"

A powerful prayer to pray:
Hallelujah, Lord. I'm opening my heart today and pushing discouragement out. I'm taking in excitement from Your Spirit. Something wonderful is about to happen. You have been working together something good. I'm about to receive a gift that will help and fulfill me. In the name of Jesus. Amen.

NOTES:

_____

_____

_____

Day 53

A Step of Trust

What does trust look like?

A man tells how when his two daughters were small, one of the things they loved to do was to climb up on a table, then as they jumped off they would shout, "Daddy, catch me!" So right away he would run and stretch out his arms to catch them before they hit the ground. He said it was amazing that they never acted as though there was any danger when they jumped off the table. If their daddy was there, they knew he would catch them. They had complete trust.

God wants us to trust Him so much that when we take a step into His will, we know His arms will be there to catch us. With complete confidence in Him, we say, "Daddy, catch me!" And we know our Daddy will be there. He will not allow us to fall and hit the ground, but we will land in His arms. When we have that kind of trust, that's when remarkable things can happen in our life.

This is what happened for the Israelites when they took a step of trust to go into the land God had promised. Over two million of them were waiting to own new property where they could build their homes and make happy lives for themselves and their children. They had waited a long time. Now what was blocking them was an overflowing, muddy, terrible Jordan River.

Then God gave the word to Joshua, their leader, that it was time to step out with trust. They would have to walk through the river and believe it would part so they could cross over on dry ground. It would take a miracle. The Jordan River was swollen because it was harvest time. There was a strong and rapid current due to the winter snows that had melted in the north. They had to have trust in God in order to confront those tough conditions and do what He had told them to do.

Think about this: trust is not a nice comfortable emotion. It pulls you up out of your comfortable seat and thrusts you into spiritual confrontation. The devil is not going to let you have faith and go easy on you. You have to be willing to be uncomfortable so you can see God's will done and experience what He has for you. Oh yes, trust is far from being dull or boring. It will wake you up! You become alert and ready.

The priests were the first ones to go into the river in front of all people, and as they stepped into that swirling muddy river, they were saying, "Daddy, catch me." Immediately, the waters became blocked upstream and the river stopped flowing. Soon, the waters disappeared and the bed of the river became dry.

As soon as the people finished crossing, and everyone was on the other shore, the river returned to its place. They trusted God to cross that river and now they definitely could trust Him to help them conquer the land that He promised to them. Their dreams were coming to pass.

That's what happens when you trust. You conquer your fears and have faith that your dream will come to pass. You're confident the Lord is there to catch you as you step out and do His will.

He will take you the way that is best for you and show you how to accomplish what's in your heart. He knows the need or pain or complication you're facing. Trust Him to show you how to pass through it and into the fulfillment of what He has for you.

Wonderful things that seem impossible can happen. Are you ready to say, "Daddy, catch me"?

A Spiritual Powerline to say out loud:
"I TAKE A STEP OF TRUST!"

A powerful prayer to pray:
Father, the conditions I'm facing are tough. But I trust You. So I step out with faith in my heart as You direct me. As I do, I say, "Daddy, catch me." And I know You will be there for me. You will part the river so I can see my desire fulfilled. In the name of Jesus. Amen.

NOTES:

_____

_____

_____

Day 54

Don't Doubt in the Drought

One of the most important truths that we can believe is that God is in control. Now it sounds real good-and-Christian to say that. "God is in control."

But I can tell you there are times my mind wants to question that; how about you? It's when you feel the rug has been pulled out from under you, or something important has been taken. Circumstances are causing you issues. There are times when you're hurting or you're down or frustrated or fed up, and it can be hard to say, "I'm sure God is in control."

When you view the situation, you might feel as if it is going to fall apart instead of being in control. But that's when God enables us to pull it together as we rely on Him. **No matter how the circumstances appear, He. Truly. Is. In. Control.**

I think of a man who had the rug pulled out from under him and he had to be convinced of this very truth to keep from being depressed or fearful about what was happening. His name was Ernie Harwell and he was the play-by-play announcer for the Detroit Tigers baseball team. He had been their announcer for thirty years. Loved his job. And the fans cherished him.

Then one day new owners took over the Detroit Tigers, and they dismissed Ernie. As a Christian, he decided to take the high road and not badmouth anyone for forcing him out. But it definitely challenged his faith.

Later he said, "I refused to allow myself to be bitter. According to Romans 8:28, God causes the circumstances of our lives to work together for good. I had an assurance that [God] was in control and I could trust Him."

There are times when *what we're sure of* is tested.

But Ernie was confident God was in control so he controlled himself and stayed out of anxiety and depression. The next season, he joined the broadcast team of the California Angels in Anaheim. Although he did well, he still missed Detroit. And the fans of Detroit missed him. In fact, they continued to demand that he be returned. Two years later, another new owner took over the Detroit Tigers and decided to reinstate Ernie. He continued to do the play-by-play broadcasting until he retired at the age of eighty-four.

God is in control no matter how it appears. Jeremiah 17:7 says, *[Most] blessed is the [one] who believes in, trusts in, and relies on the Lord, and whose hope and* **confidence the Lord is**. That says you are not only blessed but you are the MOST blessed when you have confidence in the Lord. That's where blessed assurance comes from—believing that He is in control of your life.

Because you believe, the next verse says, *You shall be like a tree planted by the waters that spreads out its roots by the river; and it shall not see and fear when heat comes; but its leaf shall be green. It shall not be anxious and full of care in the year of drought, nor shall it cease yielding fruit.*

You're as a tree planted by the waters who is so blessed that you spread out and prosper in every area. When the heat comes, you don't see it and fear it, but you believe God is taking care of you. You don't shrivel up from the drought, but your leaf is green, meaning your life is well and prosperous; you're growing in God.

You're rooted in good soil so you don't doubt in the drought. Oh yes, the drought comes, but you keep that blessed assurance inside you. That's what Ernie Harwell was determined to do. He was in a drought, but he wasn't going to doubt. He was sure God was in control and he would see the evidence of it if he had confidence in the Lord.

Don't doubt in the drought but continue to believe your life will yield fruit. You will see God bring goodness to you. When you're facing those drought conditions say, "I'm sure God is in control!" You'll be amazed what that will do for your faith to get you through.

A Spiritual Powerline to say out loud:
"GOD IS IN CONTROL!"

A powerful prayer to pray:
Lord, when a drought comes in my circumstances and the heat is on, I will not doubt. I believe You are in control. I have that blessed assurance. Therefore I will see my life prosper in every way. In the name of Jesus. Amen.

NOTES:

_____

_____

_____

Day 55

What's Your Password?

If I would ask you, "What is your password," the first thing you would probably ask me is which one. Have you noticed how many times you have to use a password each day for different things? We have them for our computers, our phones, websites, bank accounts, you name it. That's because if we want to secure our information, we have to create a password. The definition of password is a code word that gives access approval to resources.

You have a password for the spiritual part of your life also. If you want to gain access to the resources God has for you, you have to be using the right word. He has a password for miracles, answers, promotion and healing and support and growth in Him. The password is BELIEVE.

When you tell God that you believe, you open the door to everything He has for you. You demonstrate that you have faith that He will do what's in His Word and what He has put in your heart. Then that opens the way to seeing fulfillment from Him. He takes that word "believe" and He responds to it. It's the key word. So He has to hear that from you in order to start the activity of fulfilling what He wants to do. That starts the breakthrough.

Sometimes when you're trying to get into your computer account, you may forget your password. So you keep trying different things you think it may be. After several tries, if it's not correct, the system locks you out. Those wrong words you tried locked you out of what you needed to see.

Now think of that in a spiritual sense. The right spiritual password can open up and give you access to what you need. But the wrong spiritual password locks up spiritual things. Wrong words lock up your miracle. You're prevented from getting to it.

If you are so burdened or worried or fed up with how things are going, you may forget to say to God, "I believe!" Instead you may be saying things such as, "This is not going to happen. There is no sign of anything being done about this." But whatever the devil tries to put into your mind and heart, you can reject those.

There is a story of a man who learned the right password and because of it he saw a great miracle. He had come to ask Jesus to cure his boy who was possessed by a spirit, which deprived him of his ability to speak and hear. As soon as the father saw Him, he rushed up and said, *If You can do anything, do have pity on us and help us* (Mark 9:22).

Now at this point, in order to help this father, Jesus has to give him the password. It will help him open the operating system for miracles. You see God has an operating system and just as in the natural when you use a password to open the operating system, you can open God's operating system for you with the right password. When you say the word *believe* that can cause miracles to operate in your life.

So here is Jesus' response to the father after he asked Him if He can do anything. He said, *You say to Me, If You can do anything? Why, all things are possible to him who believes* (Mark 9:23)! There it is. That's the key word. All things are possible, every miracle you need, all the healing and deliverance and promotion and wisdom and guidance and growth and discipline and prosperity. Everything is possible to come to you when you BELIEVE.

So the father got the message. At once he cried out with tears, "Lord, I believe! Help my weakness of faith!" He said the word, the password. "I believe." Then he ended by adding these words expressing his human emotions, "Help my weakness of faith." Because in his heart he believed, Jesus threw open the miracle operating system and delivered that boy and made him whole again. Restored him to his father.

God is ready to raise you up to a miracle in your life. Once you say the password, He does the rest. Say right now, "Lord, I believe! Help me." Feel the power of what's happening. A breakthrough is starting. The doors to what you need are opening. You have told God you believe and now all things are possible to you. You said the password. It doesn't matter what kind of emotions or thoughts you're fighting at this moment, He knows your heart. And it's your heart that counts. From your heart you are saying, "I believe" to Him. That's what matters. It produces the miracle.

When you say, "I believe," God says, "Now, I'll do the rest."

A Spiritual Powerline to say out loud:
"I BELIEVE!"

A powerful prayer to pray:
Lord, I say to You right now from my heart, "I believe." I will not allow my emotions and thoughts to cause me to miss my miracle. All things are possible to me by faith. Now I believe You will take my faith and You will do the rest. In the name of Jesus. Amen.

NOTES:

_____

_____

_____

Day 56

It Can Change

When we are facing unwanted conditions, it's easy to go around wondering, *What if this won't change? What am I going to do?* Those thoughts drain our spirit. They pull us down. Then our attitude goes in the dumps and our thoughts convince us there's not much hope. But think what can happen if we say, "This can change! It can turn around suddenly." We hang onto that thought and believe it will in fact happen.

This is what a family had to do when they were facing a real crisis. Karen was thrilled when she found out she was going to have another baby, so she began to prepare their three-year-old son, Michael, for the day when his new sister would arrive. One of the things Michael began to do was to sing to his sister even before she was born. As he did, he began to bond with her. It was a wonderful time.

Then the day came when she was to be born, but after the birth, something went wrong. So in the hospital in Tennessee, his new sister lay there in a very serious condition. And it became worse as the days went on. There did not seem to be much hope.

When Michael found out about his baby sister, he insisted that he be able to go sing to her. Karen explained to him that she was in intensive care and children were not allowed there. But because he continued to insist, Karen decided she would find some way to get Michael up there to see the baby.

So she found a hospital scrub suit and dressed him in it; then they walked right into ICU. The head nurse could tell right away this was a child and so she roared, "Get that kid out of here now. No children are allowed in his unit." But Karen, urged on by the

Holy Spirit, turned and said to the nurse, "He is not leaving until he sings to his sister."

Michael went over to the bedside of this tiny infant trying to stay alive and he began to sing, "You are my sunshine, my only sunshine; you make me happy when skies are gray." Right away, the baby's pulse rate began to calm down and became steady. Karen began to cry as she said to Michael, "Keep singing." So he sang, "You never know, dear, how much I love you, **please don't take my sunshine away.**" His baby sister responded again and her breathing became smooth. Once again Karen told Michael to keep singing.

"The other night, dear, as I lay sleeping, I dreamed I held you in my arms." As he sang, you could see this little brother waiting for the opportunity to hold his baby sister in his arms. Suddenly, a healing rest seemed to sweep over the baby. By this time the nurse who had ordered them to go had tears flowing down her face.

The song that Michael sang from his little heart was used by God to do the job. The next day...now what did we say—it can change *suddenly*...the very next day this baby girl was well enough to go home. She went from a desperate prognosis to going home to be in the arms of her big brother.

Have faith God will turn your situation around. The breakthrough can come suddenly—whatever the condition may be. I see this happen for so many people who contact us to agree in prayer with them. I think of one Partner who faced such financial need that it seemed she and her family would be bogged down with need forever. But they thought, *What if it turned around all of a sudden?* That's what happened.

After we prayed and stood in faith together, they were able to sell their old car for more money than they expected. Then they received a check for a large sum of money from the government that was unexpected. On top of all of that, her husband received a raise and it was the first he had had in over two years. They found a new car to buy for half the price, with the exact color and features they desired.

When God sees that you believe your situation can change, that activates the turnaround. So, expect to see it happen...suddenly!

A Spiritual Powerline to say out loud:
"THIS IS GOING TO CHANGE!"

A powerful prayer to pray:
Lord, I believe You will turn my situation around. I have faith that something is beginning to happen now! And I will see it change... suddenly! I praise You for what is about to happen by Your power. In the name of Jesus. Amen.

NOTES:

_____

_____

_____

Day 57

Get on the Wall

When you need a solution to what you're facing do you ever think, *I don't understand what's happening? Where do I go from here?*

That's when you have to follow by faith. Rest assured that God has the answer for what you're facing right now. He has a plan for the need. However, you have to arrive at a certain place in your thinking before those plans can be shown to you and understood. The answer may not be in your realm of experience right now. God is not keeping the answer from you to torment you. But He will reveal it to you day by day as you follow Him by faith.

Think of it like this. Todd Skinner was a champion rock climber and became one of the most achieved climbers ever. The rocks he conquered were amazing. But there was one that was especially dangerous called Trango Tower. It's the highest freestanding spire and has a near vertical drop—straight up. Smooth. Pure granite. So it's very hard to get a hold and go up. It is located in a tough region in an area north of Pakistan.

When Todd and his group decided to take on the challenge of climbing it, he was no novice. He had conquered many others, but this was going to be the hardest. So he started his planning— the travel, all the permits they needed, equipment and tents and supplies. Then he was ready!

But regardless of how much preparation the team made, they did not fully understand the challenge until they got there and stood in front of the biggest, tallest, and smoothest rock wall they had ever seen. The reality of the challenge hit them. That's when Todd realized there was only one thing to do. They had to go ahead and "get on the wall." They had done all the preparation they could and now they had come to the point that *on that rock wall* was the only place the answers could be found of how to get up it.

So, they began their climb, and after sixty days, they reached the summit. Despite the years of preparation and training, much of what they learned about going up the Trango Tower was only discovered after they got on the wall.

That group could not know all of the answers for going up the rock until they got on it. **Before we can experience God's answers, we have to get on the wall.** Some things have to be discovered after we are there. So we have to follow by faith. Day by day.

That's the way it was for Abraham. When God was urging him to go to a land with which he was not familiar, Abraham had to follow by faith. He had to get on the wall so to speak. Because he did, he became one of the most blessed men of his time. (Refs. Genesis 12 and Hebrews 11.)

There are answers for you.

There are plans.

There are experiences God has designed.

Be willing to follow by faith. Get on the wall. Take a step at a time and watch as His plans are revealed to you. They will unfold into the great wonders in your heart.

A Spiritual Powerline to say out loud:
"I FOLLOW BY FAITH!"

A powerful prayer to pray:
Lord, there are things I don't understand about what I'm facing. But I know You have the answers. You have a plan for me. So I'm going to follow by faith. I'm going to get on the wall and climb this mountain. Each day I will take the steps I need to take. Now, I have great joy knowing that I will see Your plans for me unfold. In the name of Jesus. Amen.

NOTES:

_____

_____

_____

Day 58

Lay It Down

If you are as I am, there have been times that you have lain in bed and even though you were supposed to be resting, you were thinking about something. But there comes a time when we must lay it down. I know this is hard to do because of lifestyles today. There is so much technology available that we can find ourselves using it continually. And of course there are more serious things that absorb us. Incidents that have happened in relationships, situations in our family or work or with our financial well-being. Our health. Duties. Desires unfulfilled.

That's why God says in Psalm 37 that we are to roll ever care of our load on Him and trust Him to bring our desire to pass. That means you must...lay it down. Don't keep picking it up, but move away from it so God can refresh your emotions and mind. Be confident that He will help you. If not, you can end up with more issues or problems.

Think of it this way. Many orthopedic surgeons are noticing a trend in young athletes being injured more often. The reason? No time off. They are pushing too hard. They're playing some kind of sport all year and so muscles and joints can't recover from the micro trauma that occurs during practice and play. They simply are not laying it down when they should, in order to keep their body healthy.

Next time you're holding onto something too long and you're not resting and rolling it on God, remind yourself of the possible repercussions mentally and emotionally and eventually in your health—which then can affect your relationships, decision-making, and the ability to be happy. Say to yourself, *It's time to lay it down.* Then allow God to renew you and show you the answers for your desires.

A Spiritual Powerline to say out loud:
"I LAY IT DOWN!"

A powerful prayer to pray:
Dear Lord, I'm glad You're there to handle everything that concerns me. Help me to stop rolling those things around inside me and instead roll them on You. I do that now in the name of Jesus. I

lay it down. You're going to see me through everything that I face. So I trust You. I rest in You. Amen.

NOTES:

_____

_____

_____

Go to God

All throughout God's Word, He emphasizes how you are to rely on Him. Go to Him for your fulfillment, for your needs to be met, for your joy and happiness, for EVERYTHING. When you do that, you will see the power and beauty of what He has planned for your life. God is there for you. Now, depend on Him. Look to Him as the answer, the source. Worship Him as your creator and provider. When you see Him as your all-in-all, then you can see a breakthrough.

Day 59

Break the Grip

At times we may feel we're struggling against circumstances. Almost as though they're trying to take us under. Instead of becoming tired from the struggle, we need to make sure we are looking to the Lord for the way out.

When a man named Jimmy was on vacation with his family in Mexico, he and his son, Davey, were playing in the ocean while some of his family members were on the beach. Suddenly, a very strong rip current started sweeping Davey out to sea. Rip currents, or riptides as some people call them, are hard to get away from because you don't know where they're coming from.

Jimmy immediately started trying to help his son back to shore, but even though he is an Olympic decathlete, soon he was being swept away in the current also. He knew that in a few minutes both he and his son would drown. He tried to scream, but his family couldn't hear him. He began to have a chilling thought of how his wife and daughters were going to have to have a double funeral.

Suddenly, his cousin saw what was happening and understood something about how rip currents worked. If you try to struggle against the current, you will go under. In order to swim out of it, you have to swim *with* the current and go parallel to the shore, not directly into it. It's called breaking the grip of the rip. So the cousin walked out into the water where he knew there was a sandbar. He lifted his hands and said to Jimmy and Davey, "You come to me. You come to me." As soon as they started swimming the direction where he was instead of trying to swim against the current, they were soon out of trouble and safe.

Can't you hear the Father's words to you as the rip current of circumstances tries to take you under?

"You come to Me. You come to Me."

He is showing you the right direction to go so you can get out of the trouble and be safe. Instead of struggling against problems or hurt or disappointment, go towards the Lord. *That breaks the grip of the rip.*

Hear God's heart calling you today. As you swim towards Him, He will lift you out of the swirling circumstances and into His arms. And once you're in the hands of the Protector, you will come out just fine. Delivered and successful.

If it had not been the Lord Who was on our side—then the waters would have overwhelmed us and swept us away, the torrent would have gone over us. Our help is in the name of the Lord, Who made heaven and earth (Psalm 124:1, 4, 8).

A Spiritual Powerline to say out loud:
"I BREAK THE GRIP OF THE RIP!"

A powerful prayer to pray:
O Father, I hear Your heart calling, "Come to Me." So I reach out to You today. I will not struggle against the circumstances, but I follow Your direction. Show me what to do, the words to speak, the actions to take. Lift me out of the swirling circumstances and into safety and victory. In the name of Jesus. Amen.

NOTES:

_____

_____

_____

Day 60

Soaking

To soak means to become saturated. When you soak in the presence of God, you're saturated with power, love, and the insight God has to give to you.

That means you don't just dip your finger into God's presence. You come face-to-face with the One who loves you, and you speak to Him from your heart. You hear and adhere to His words coming into your spirit as you are with Him.

If you just go into His presence from time to time and only dip your finger in God's presence, that is the level of benefit you will receive. A bit of blessing. A drop of deliverance. A spoonful of spiritual renewal.

But if you need to see God really move in your circumstances with a breakthrough, you have to soak in Him so He can fill your being in a greater way. That's when you become so saturated with His Spirit that the circumstances that have tried to take hold on your life must release their hold.

Here's a good way to think about this. A man took a trip through the Burma jungle with a guide. As he saw all the wonders, he was thrilled with the adventure. At one point they had to wade through a shallow river to continue their journey. When they came out of it, the traveler realized that he had leeches attached all over him. He couldn't stand it.

The first thing he wanted to do is what all of us would want to do—he started to grab the leeches to pull them off. But his guide immediately stopped him. He explained that if he pulled a leech away, what remained would be a tiny piece of it under his skin which would cause infection. So how was he to get rid of them?

He had to soak in a warm balsam bath. As he soaked, the leeches would have to release their hold on his body.

As you immerse yourself in God, you're bathing in the balsam of His anointing which heals and soothes and restores. Just as those leeches fell off that man's body, the leeches in your life will have to fall off. Instead of trying to pull the circumstances off by your own power so that small pieces are left and become infected, when you go to God, He doesn't allow even a trace of the trouble to remain.

Come into God's presence today and say to Him, "Lord, I'm coming to sit here and soak in Your presence until these leeches— the needs and challenges—release their hold on me. I'm not going to try to pull them off by my own power. And I'm not going to carry them around anymore. These bloodsucking problems are going to be released by Your power!"

When you soak in God's presence, what is trying to hang onto you will no longer be able to hang on. Don't just dip your finger in God's presence but soak and experience wonderful results.

A Spiritual Powerline to say out loud:
"I SOAK IN GOD'S PRESENCE!"

A powerful prayer to pray:
Lord, I come today to soak in Your presence. As I do, I believe for You to force the circumstances that are leeching onto me to release their hold. Now, fill me. Transform my vision in Your presence. I believe something great is starting now. In the name of Jesus. Amen.

NOTES:

_____

_____

_____

Day 61

Camp on God's Doorstep

If you want something very much, you go where you need to go in order to get it. For instance, on the news we see the lines of people that form every time a new iPhone is introduced. Those people come to camp out. Sometimes we see lines of people in front of movie theaters or concerts. Or how many times have you stood in line at a restaurant where you wanted to eat? We get in line because there is something we really want.

Now, are we willing to do the same thing when we want help from the Lord? Will we camp out on His doorstep? "I'm here, Lord, to be with You, to hear Your voice, to feel Your presence." The Lord loves to hear that from us. He desires our fellowship. He sees that we want Him more than anything else. We're there to look to Him for our guidance and help. In other words, we go where God is. That's what it means to camp out on His doorstep.

It's during that time that we can receive what we need from the Lord. We find our faith being built up to believe a relationship can in fact be restored. We can get rid of this sickness or pain or affliction. All of a sudden, the revelation hits us that it's possible to be debt-free.

We think, *I serve a big enough God that can turn around this circumstance. He can solve this issue. Yes, my dream can be fulfilled. Things can be better.*

Our spirit becomes renewed to believe. We're camping on God's doorstep and He knows we mean business about receiving from Him.

We see how this happened for a man in the Bible called Naaman. (Ref. II Kings 5.) As the commander of the Army of Syria, he had everything going for him—success, prestige, honor, and blessing. But he needed healing in his body from leprosy. One day a maid to his wife mentioned that if Naaman would go to Elisha, the prophet in Samaria, he could be healed of his leprosy. That's what he finally determined to do. He got away from the hopelessness and went where there was hope. If you need restoration, help, provision, or a cure—in some way you need something to be made better in your life, then go where there is hope.

The Bible says, *So Naaman came with his horses and chariots and stopped at Elisha's **door*** (II Kings 5:9). He's on the right doorstep now—the doorstep of God. Elisha told him to go dip in the Jordan River seven times and he would come up with pure skin, completely healed. At first Naaman rebelled because he didn't want to do something so humble as dip in the muddy Jordan River. Then he decided to show that he meant business and he went to the Jordan to do what Elisha had instructed. Every time he went under the water, he was getting closer to his need being met. Down. Up. Down. Up. On the seventh time, he got his breakthrough. The Bible says he came up restored and clean.

Show God you mean business. Don't leave until you receive what you came after. Camp out on His doorstep to receive your miracle blessing from Him.

A Spiritual Powerline to say out loud:
"I MEAN BUSINESS!"

A powerful prayer to pray:
Lord, I know You are the One who can supply all I need and give me the help I must have. Therefore I'm camping out on Your doorstep. I come into Your presence now and seek Your guidance. You are my hope. And I know I will receive what I came for. In the name of Jesus. Amen.

NOTES:

_____

_____

_____

Day 62

You Are in the Hands of God

You are not in the hands of the problem or the challenge you are facing; you're in God's hands. And what put you in His hands? Your worship!

If you have been worshiping, then when you look out over the issues and needs and disappointment, out of your spirit will come, "My God will take care of this for me. He will send me a breakthrough."

This is what the people of a small town on the Austrian border did. Napoleon had stationed a huge army on the mountains just above the town in order to attack and take it over. So the town council had a meeting to try to decide what they would do. They could try to defend themselves or they could wave the white flag. Either way, the outcome did not seem it would be good.

When a hard situation is facing us, it can seem as though the outcome will not be good no matter what we do. But God tells us that's the time to worship Him. **Through worship, we put ourselves in His hands and that's when we can see His faithfulness go into action for us.**

So these townspeople gathered in the church and the minister got up and said, "Friends, we have been counting on our own strength, and apparently that has failed. Let us just ring the bells, have our worship as usual, and put the matter in God's hands." So that's what they decided to do. They rang the church bells and had their worship service. While they were worshiping, the enemy heard the loud sounds of the bells ringing and thought that was the townspeople celebrating because the Austrian army must have arrived during the night to defend the town. Before the people even finished their worship, Napoleon's army had picked up their weapons and gone away.

My Friend, before you even leave your time of worship with God, the enemy is already leaving. I just love that. As you worship the Lord, you're activating His faithfulness and before you walk away from that time, the enemy is already walking away. He must! Because he knows you are in God's hands. The Lord will sustain and defend you. That's because your worship caused you to look to Him for your help and your defense and not to yourself. You believed He would come through and you were in His care and power.

Second Chronicles 16 describes how *the eyes of the Lord run to and fro throughout the whole earth to show Himself strong in behalf of those whose hearts are blameless toward Him* (v. 9).

Who are the ones whose hearts are blameless toward God? People who are perfect? Well, that leaves out you and me. No, those whose hearts are blameless toward God are those who are worshiping Him! That's us! God's eyes are open, watching, and He is waiting to show Himself strong for you—the one who worships and has your heart turned toward Him.

That's why you have to continue your worship—continue to seek God. You must be reminded that you are in His hands, so you can stand in the face of the enemy. And that's when the efforts of the enemy take a dive. No matter how much bigger they seem than you are, the Lord overrides what comes against you when you look to Him.

Oh yes, you are in the hands of God—the best place to be!

A Spiritual Powerline to say out loud:
"I'M IN GOD'S HANDS!"

A powerful prayer to pray:
Lord, I worship You! As I do, I put myself in Your hands. You know everything that concerns me. And You're ready to show Yourself strong in my behalf. So I believe You will take care of me. You will bring me to victory. In the name of Jesus. Amen.

NOTES:

_____

_____

_____

Day 63

Let the Love of God Change It

When you worship, you connect with God. And when you make contact with God, you make contact with love and power.

Just think of the times you've been in His presence and as you worshiped, your heart was filled with love toward Him. But it cannot compare with the love and affection you receive from Him in return. It has life and acceptance in it. You are lifted through it. God gives you what you need to have the strength to go on.

In this harsh world, without feeling His love, we shrivel. We can't grow. **Our vitality, our very life is tied to having the love of God connect with us.**

You have to feel love from Him and know that He is there. Then it will remain with you throughout the day so you can walk into what you need to do and face trials and have the strength and understanding to experience victory. The love of God is what will minister to you in the toughest of times as you worship.

There was a couple who was going through a very tough time but everything changed when the love of God came into the circumstances. A doctor tells the story of how he was standing at a hospital bed visiting this young woman for whom he had just performed surgery. She had a tumor in her cheek and in order to remove that tumor he had to sever a facial nerve that connected to the muscles of her mouth. Because the nerve had to be cut, it had caused a deformity in her mouth. It made it crooked.

So the doctor was on one side of the bed and her husband was on the other side. When the woman saw the results of the surgery on her mouth, she asked the doctor, "Will my mouth always be this way?" The doctor slowly said, "Yes." So she just slightly nodded her head but didn't say anything.

At that very moment, the love of God entered into that situation. When her husband saw her disappointment, he smiled and said, "I like it; it's kind of cute." Then he bent down and kissed her crooked mouth by twisting his lips to match the way her lips were now. He was showing her that he still could kiss her just fine, and the love he had for her had not diminished. The doctor said he just stood there silent. **He knew he had witnessed the love of God.**

We experience that divine love when we connect with God. He knows we're not perfect just as her mouth was not perfect. But He still kisses our life. He bends down to where we are in all of our problems or weaknesses or pain, and He connects His love with us—right where we are.

That's what you experience when you come into worship and develop that love relationship with Him. But you can only develop that relationship if you are willing to make contact with Him in worship. Just as that married couple had to desire to be with each other and to connect in their hearts, that's how it is with God and you. You desire to be with Him as He desires to be with you.

When you worship Him, you feel His touch in your spirit; you hear His voice in your heart. That gives you life! He tells you how much He cares for you because you're with Him and so you can sense that. Maybe you don't hear words from God, but there is a sense of love that comes into your being.

Let me tell you, **what happens in your worship time cannot be taken from you.** It's going to help sustain you and strengthen you. It clears out impossible type thinking. Your thoughts are transformed to think in terms of God's bigness instead of your smallness. God becomes BIG to you. Worship puts things into perspective so you can grow in your understanding of Him.

During that time that you are with Him, the Lord takes His hand and touches you with compassion and care; He speaks to you from the love in His heart for you. Oh can't you just feel that?

As you worship Him, He hovers over you and you feel the touch of love and hear the care and compassion coming from His Spirit into you.

Connect your heart with God today and feel the love He has for you.

A Spiritual Powerline to say out loud:
"I WORSHIP YOU, GOD!"

A powerful prayer to pray:
God, I want to connect with You today! As I worship You, I feel Your love and affection. You are my life, and You strengthen me so I will experience victory. In Jesus' name. Amen.

NOTES:

_____

_____

_____

Day 64

Satisfy Your Hunger

We have hunger for a purpose. It drives us to get food so our bodies can be nourished. The hungrier we allow ourselves to become, the more desperate we become to get food. In fact, if we are hungry enough, we will grab just about anything—even substitutes.

A research group discovered that the longer we go with our hunger *not* being filled, the more apt we are to take anything just to make us feel that we got *something* even if it's not food! They did an experiment in which they took two adult groups and told them not to eat for four hours. After the time was up, they took one group and gave them as much cake as they desired. The second group received nothing to eat. Then just before both groups left, they gave each person a binder clip from an office supply place. Just a normal office binder clip. They were told they could take as many of these as they felt they needed.

What was interesting was that the members of the group who were still hungry took home seventy percent more clips than the group that had their hunger satisfied with cake. Hunger was such a driving force that even though they could not satisfy themselves with food, they had to have *something!* So they grabbed what was offered to them—binder clips from an office supply place!

Think of spiritual hunger being the same way as when your body is hungry. When you're not feeding your spiritual hunger with God, you will start accepting substitutes. If you get busy or distracted and you're missing meals with God, then you may start to grab for fast food.

It can come in the form of excessive TV or social media, or running here and there, or if spiritually starved, people can go to more destructive things such as drugs, alcohol, bad habits, pornography, eating disorders, overworking, and wrong relationships.

We substitute a missed meal with God in small and big ways. All the while, He is near us showing that He has something great prepared for our spiritual meal and it will fill our hunger with good things which will grow us and help us. We can eat spiritual food from Him that blesses and strengthens.

If we ignore this basic spiritual need, that's when we can give up what is rightfully ours from God. Think how Esau did this. He stayed out in the field too long hunting for game and got to the place he would do anything for food. When he came upon his brother, Jacob, and smelled lentil soup cooking, he was so hungry that he was willing to make a deal with Jacob for a bowl of soup. He ended up giving him his birthright as the firstborn and the blessing that went with it. Because of hunger, the Bible says Esau scorned his birthright as beneath his notice. (Ref. Genesis 25.)

When you stay out in "the field" too long, then you're going to get so spiritually hungry that you may give up your blessings. Have your meal time with God. That's when you gain hope that things will work out. As you eat with Him, you are filled with faith. You can make it through what confronts you and not only that, but you can see God take care of your desires and dreams. Don't miss a meal with God! Instead of grabbing substitutes, fill yourself with what will sustain and help you receive all that is destined for you.

A Spiritual Powerline to say out loud:
"GOD FILLS MY HUNGER WITH GOOD THINGS!"

A powerful prayer to pray:
Oh God, I come to You now to have a spiritual meal. I want to sit down and talk with You and feed on Your presence and Your Word. Satisfy the longing of my heart to feel Your love and comfort. Fill my thoughts with the good words You have about my life. And give

me the power I need to see Your miracles. I don't want to miss one meal with You. Please fill my hunger. In the name of Jesus. Amen.

NOTES:

_____

_____

_____

Day 65

Every Detail

In Psalm 8, David asked God a very revealing question. He had just viewed the heavens and seen the moon and the stars, and the expanse of the universe. It was beyond what one small human could take in.

So in the midst of being awed by what God had created and seeing the works of His hands, David said, *What is man that You are mindful of him, and the son of man that You care for him?* (Ref. Psalm 8:4.) Another translation says, *Why are people even important to You? Why do You take care of human beings?* (Ref. Psalm 8:4 NCV.) "I mean, God, if You have created such tremendous beautiful awesome stuff, that's big and expansive, why would You bother with a small speck such as I?"

To be mindful of someone means you're attentive, you observe their life; you heed whatever they say and do. That's what God is doing. He is observing you and regarding your life. He's very conscious of everything about you.

Now, why is that so important? Because until you fully realize and accept that, you won't be able to have the faith you need to receive all He has for you. **It's easier to believe God will act in your behalf when you know that He is aware of what's happening and is involved with everything about you.**

You can accomplish more and receive more. Your life will open up and blossom in a greater way because you sense God of heaven watching over you. He delights in the details of your life—things that we might assume would be too unimportant for God to mess with. Yet, at times He does something to remind us of how much He's involved in the details of our life.

He made this so real to a man who had a financial need when he was a pastor. He was pioneering a church and had five kids at the time, so you can understand how he had financial constraints. One of the needs his family had was for a car so they could replace the old one they had. They had to have something better.

One day when his mother was praying concerning this need, she called and asked him to give her the details of what kind of car he wanted. He didn't think it would hurt to tell her so he went down a list of what he desired in the car. In just a few days, his mother called him again and said God had shown her the car they were going to receive. It was a white van with a blue stripe. It had seven seats for the entire family, a good paint job.

Then she went down all the details of the car. Also, it was going to be a bargain buy. Then just before she hung up she added that one other thing God had shown her was there was going to be a small amount of red dust somewhere in the car because of where it had been.

Well, after he heard his mother say all of this, he laughed to himself and thanked her. He didn't have the money to buy the kind of car his mother had described. It was out of his reach. Then a short time after this, he found a van for sale. He decided to go see it, even though he thought it would be too much. When he got there, you guessed it. That van was...

White with a blue stripe.

Seven seats.

Good paint job.

A bargain buy.

And as he continued looking over the car, he found a bit of red dust.

God delights in the details of your life. You can believe it when He says in Philippians 4 that He will supply all your need according to His riches in glory by Christ Jesus. What part of your need will He take care of? That scripture said ALL. Big stuff, small stuff, and in between.

Don't stop short and think this is just for material things. When God says in His Word that He'll supply all your need, He means in every area of your life. He knows every struggle you have, every desire and dream, the problems and difficulties and disappointment. He's mindful of it all, and He will supply it all as you believe that you have a Lord who is involved in your life.

Now believe that He is going to come to you very soon and show how mindful He is of you. He wants to increase your faith to believe for a breakthrough for all that He has for you.

A Spiritual Powerline to say out loud:
"GOD WILL TAKE CARE OF EVERY DETAIL!"

A powerful prayer to pray:
Lord, I believe You will take care of every detail of (now fill in the name for what you are believing). You care about me and every need I have. You delight in my life. I'm expecting wonderful things from Your hand. In the name of Jesus. Amen.

NOTES:

_____

_____

_____

Make Your Waiting Work for You

When you enter a time of waiting for your desire to be fulfilled, it can be hard to keep faith that it will happen. So it's important during this time that you don't just endure, but you make your waiting time work for you. That means to recognize great things can be formed and grow and flourish as you wait. Waiting can be a powerful tool in your hand and heart. God is doing something! So believe it will be worth the wait when you see the breakthrough.

Day 66

Wait for the Maple Syrup

There are some things that are worth waiting for. We soon find that out when we desire something so much, but we see that we can't have it right away. That's when we have to make a decision if we will give up, or take a substitute we really don't want, or go through the process of waiting.

What we don't realize sometimes is that something good is happening in that process if we will go through it—it's a time when God is preparing us for something great ahead. We just have to give it some time. Think of it in this way—you're waiting for the best, the real maple syrup. Have you heard how maple syrup is produced? It's a picture of what may be happening to you right now.

First, the maple trees have to be tapped and buckets are hung under the taps. Then they start to drip sap. Not pouring, but dripping, and just a small portion at a time. What comes out is thin and not brown as you see in the stores. Also there isn't much sweetness to it, in fact you wouldn't even think it was syrup if you saw it and tasted it. That's how it all starts. This is such a long process, that it takes fifty trees to yield thirty to forty gallons of sap.

Then once the buckets are full, the contents are put into a large bin over an open fire. When it starts to boil, that reduces the water content and then the sugar becomes concentrated. After some time of going through this process, the syrup has a good flavor and has developed the brown color that we think of when we see maple syrup. But we're still not finished.

At this point it's strained so all the impurities are removed, then reheated, packaged, and prepared for distribution. So out of thirty to forty gallons of sap, we only get one gallon of pure maple syrup. What had to happen? **You had to give it some time if you wanted the gooood stuff.** Or you can take sugar water instead of actual maple syrup.

The best has to go through the grooming process so it comes out what God intends for it to be. If you want that and no imitation, then you're going to have to give it some time. If you take on something too early, then it's going to be as the sap was—just a hint of what it needs to be. It hasn't finished developing. **You see, even though it may be uncomfortable, God knows what He's doing in the preparation process. He's getting us ready for what is ahead. Our breakthrough.**

That's why the scripture in Galatians 6:9 tells us that if we keep doing what is right—in other words going through the process of preparation and continue to obey God, then at the appointed time, we will reap and enjoy what we've been working towards. Praying for. Believing and having faith for. But notice that scripture says that it's *in due time*, at the season which has been appointed. You have to give it some time. **Let your efforts and your faith and prayers blossom and grow.** You want what you desire to flourish and be all that God intends for it to be.

You may be having faith for a new job, a new house, or you have a desire to gain some new education or go into a new field of endeavor—allow God to guide you through that process so that you get the real maple syrup. You don't want a friendship or to get married to someone who is not your maple syrup. Give it some time. This is true for everything you're after. You can see God produce what you're believing for in your finances or for that property to sell or for a project to go well at your work. Don't give up on your health until you have what you need. Don't send that manuscript off to be published until you've got maple syrup, not sugar water.

God has a grooming process that we must experience at times in order to allow things to grow. But it will be worth it when we see the results. Then we'll have the real deal.

So give it some time—He is preparing you and preparing the conditions to bless you. And He will give you the grace you need for the grooming. **Grace for the grooming.** So you don't faint but continue to do what is right so you can reap. Then one day... you will see something wonderful and fulfilling. It will grow and blossom and flourish into that for which you've been waiting.

A Spiritual Powerline to say out loud:
"I'M WAITING FOR THE BEST!"

A powerful prayer to pray:
Lord, I know You are preparing the best for me. So I'm going to keep doing what is right and reap what is promised. I have Your grace to help me wait during this grooming time. I'm waiting for the maple syrup! In the name of Jesus. Amen.

NOTES:

_____

_____

_____

Day 67

When You're Out of Options

Whatever you need, God has it. And it has already been prepared for you. That's the cool thing—it's already prepared.

You know how when you receive something from a delivery truck, it wasn't put on that truck two minutes before you received it. It had been loaded up and was already on its way.

Well, God's answers have been loaded up for you! They are on the truck! They're being shipped! He knows just what you need, and He's going to make sure it's delivered on time. God promises in Hebrews 4:16 that you'll receive help in good time for every need. Appropriate help and well-timed, coming just when you need it—when you're out of options.

A couple by the name of Francis and Edith Schaeffer knew how it felt to run out of options. God had called them to go to Europe to start Bible classes and camps for boys and girls and to write Bible studies for adults.

One day as they were living in Switzerland, they converted an important person in their community to become a Christian. When the authorities of the community found out, they were not happy, and since this was back in 1955, they were able to pressure the Schaeffers to get out of town. In fact, they gave them an ultimatum. It came at a bad time because one of their children had come down with polio and another child had rheumatic fever. There they were, without much money, trying to make financial arrangements to rent or buy a house somewhere else.

Edith decided to go out and try to find a home even though it was during a snowstorm. Time was running out to find a place to live. She felt like Joseph and Mary trying to find an inn. They were out of options!

But finally she found a house and inquired about the cost per month. When the owner told her how expensive it was, she just broke down and cried. You know how that desperate feeling is!

When she turned to go, she knew they only had until the next morning—that was how long the authorities had given them. They were running out of time. As she was walking home, a real estate agent stopped her and told her about a cottage that was for sale. Edith rushed to see the house and as soon as she did, she knew it was the answer. But the story wasn't over. In order to get that house, they had to have a big sum of money before ten o'clock the next morning! Nevertheless, the Schaeffers knew their God could deliver. The next morning a letter was delivered before ten o'clock and in it was a check for the exact amount they needed.

The devil may have been pushing them out, but God had a better place for them go. Even though they didn't have the resources they needed, those showed up on time. **God already had a letter on its way to them with a check in it.** And after they moved into their home, both their children recovered. God delivers! Their ministry took off from that point on and both Francis and Edith wrote books that sold millions of copies, and they began a publishing firm for the Gospel.

If you need a big answer, if you need someone to assist you with something right away, if your gas tank is near empty, or you need some kind of resource, expect delivery on time from God. The assets that are necessary, the time you must have, the healing or relief, any kind of resources—**God knows how to get what you need to you in the right way. Trust Him to do it His way. Your part is to believe for delivery on time!**

A Spiritual Powerline to say out loud:
"MY ANSWER IS ON THE WAY!"

A powerful prayer to pray:
Lord, thank You for encouraging me today. You have reassured me that You've already made provision for what I need. So by my faith I reach out to receive it. I know it will be delivered on time. In the name of Jesus. Amen.

NOTES:

_____

_____

_____

Day 68

Your Springtime Is Coming

You know how it is in the wintertime. Outside the grass and trees seem to have died and have no beauty. It can be hard to imagine how it used to be when we had weather that was warmer. We can't wait until the days are sunshiny and it feels good to walk outside and enjoy activities outdoors. So during the wintertime we cling to the fact that we know spring is coming.

That's how it is with our circumstances of life. We hit the wintertime. Just as grass and trees seem to die, our situation can seem to be dead and have no hope of recovery. We can't find a way to see the answers or our dreams fulfilled or to have needs met. That's when we have to rely on what we believe. **Sometimes that's all you have in the wintertime of conditions—your faith. But that's enough!**

You can have faith that works for you. It rises up in the wintertime and fills your heart with the belief that spring is coming. It helps you in the midst of those circumstances which appear dead. How does it do that? Faith looks for life! It doesn't go toward death, meaning no hope and no answer. It shows you where *life* is in your conditions. Something is stirring! There's life going on in the midst of what seems to be dying. Then you begin to see how God is moving in a great way to change things.

So it's important that when you're in the wintertime, you allow faith to work for you. Otherwise, you may lose hope or take an action that will delay or stop your springtime. Remember that a new time is coming. Say this to yourself. Say, *A new time is coming.* God is preparing your spring, so use your faith to be ready for it. It will help you see the life He is producing in your hopes and desires.

This is something a young boy learned from his father because of what happened one winter. He and his dad went out on their land to get some firewood. So as soon as his father found a dead tree, he cut it down and chopped it into firewood. Then they returned to the house. However, that spring, when he and his dad were in the same place where that tree had been, there were new shoots sprouting all around the trunk. They realized then the tree was not dead when he cut it down. It just appeared that way.

So the father said, "I thought for sure it was dead. The leaves had dropped in the wintertime. It was so cold the twigs snapped as if there was no life left in the tree. But now I see there was still life at the tap root." Then he turned to his son and said to him. "Bob, don't forget this important lesson. Never cut a tree down in the wintertime. Never make a negative decision in the low time. Wait. Be patient. Spring will come."

Are you seeing conditions that appear to be as dead and hopeless as that tree in the wintertime? Even though it's wintertime in your circumstances, remember this—that does not mean the dream is dead. The tree is still alive. Don't cut down your tree! In other words, don't stop having faith for what you want to see God do.

Matthew 10 tells us to have faith so that when we pray we will see the dead raised. There may be some dead things in your life that need to be raised. That man saw the tree and thought for sure it was dead because it had dropped leaves. It gave every appearance of having no more hope to provide shade and beauty for them.

Every appearance may seem to have no more hope to provide you beauty and joy and the assistance you need. But just as that father said: Be patient. Spring is coming.

Use your faith to help you be patient and positive in the wintertime when things appear so bad. It's with your faith that you'll be able to look for life and see it come. If that father would have had faith that the tree was not dead, he would have looked more for signs of life before cutting it down. When you don't have faith that something is working, then **you stop looking for signs**

of what God is doing. You don't look for life. You think there's no activity so there must be no life. Then you miss the signs that God sends to show you that He is working.

When you have faith, you see changes start to happen. The work God was doing underground is now popping up and showing wonderful and satisfying blessings for which you are waiting. Remember, keep watching for signs of life. Your spring is coming!

A Spiritual Powerline to say out loud:
"MY SPRINGTIME IS COMING!"

A powerful prayer to pray:
Lord, I know You're working even though I cannot see You. So though I face wintertime conditions, I refuse to cut down my hopes. I'm about to witness a bursting forth of new life. So I wait. I am patient. I know my springtime is about here. In the name of Jesus. Amen.

NOTES:

_____

_____

_____

Day 69

On the Altar

You may be burning inside to experience what is in your heart. You may wonder, *Why don't I have what God has planned for me? Why am I not fulfilling what I feel I'm supposed to be doing?*

You are in the time of the sacrifice of waiting. Even though the anointing of God is upon you to receive what He has for you, there is a time that precedes that anointing being expressed in your life. It requires sacrifice.

This was the "time" that David was experiencing. The prophet Samuel had been instructed by God to go to the house of Jesse, David's father, to anoint the next King of Israel. Saul had been King but was now rejected by God because of his disobedience, and therefore it was time for someone else to walk in their anointing. So Samuel went to anoint that person.

Then as Jesse brought before him all of his sons, most of them had the appearance of a king. The stereotype—impressive, tall, capable. As Samuel would go up to each one of them, he would think, *This is the Lord's anointed.* But God said no to them all. So Samuel asked Jesse if this was everyone, and he was told there was one more. The youngest. He was out in the field. Tending the sheep. "You wouldn't want him. He doesn't have the right appearance."

In spite of that, Samuel told Jesse to have David come in. As soon as he walked in the door, Samuel knew that even though he didn't have the best appearance, he had the anointing. God spoke to the prophet and said, *Arise, anoint him; this is he* (I Samuel 16:12).

My Friend, you may not have the *appearance*, but you have the *anointing!* And that's what counts. God has skipped over others and anointed you to do what's in your heart. You're the one chosen for what He has for you.

You are the one to fill that position, to say that word to a person, to use your gift in a special area, to pull your family together, to keep them together, or to demonstrate peace in the world of strife. You are the one anointed to produce what will help so many people.

God depends on you to make that money, heal that wound, discover that answer, have faith to receive that blessing, that healing. You can manage a team, see the need met, love others, build or restore.

You're the one who knows the anointing God has put upon you. Now you must walk into it. That's the only way you're going to be fulfilled in your heart.

But it's going to take sacrifice.

Satan can't stand it when God puts His hand on you,

when He pours the oil of anointing on your head,

when He enables you and gives you gifts and talents,

when He calls you forth to be blessed and favored.

The devil hates it so much that he sends his forces to try to snuff out that anointing. That's where the sacrifice comes in. Will you give up when the attacks of the enemy come? When things aren't going the way you desire? It's hard. The enemy tries to destroy your efforts.

So you sacrifice and keep doing what you know to do! When you do, Satan cannot snuff out your anointing. Because David was willing to stay on the altar of sacrifice and wait and go through the difficulties, the day came when Saul was removed, and the people crowned David as their King.

You're aware of what kind of sacrifice you have to make in order to walk in that anointing. You feel it. You see it. And you're experiencing it. But don't miss out on seeing the miracles God can do for you and through you because you have to sacrifice. He will give you the strength to do it.

Times may get tough. **You may feel that your entire being is up on that altar. You're being sacrificed.** You want to squirm off the altar. It's getting too hot. Too hard. During those times, think of this—your sacrifice prepares you. It is going up before God. It rises before Him as a precious aroma. He sees all you're doing. He knows what you had to give up. And now you are set up. Set up for the miracles He has prepared.

So be encouraged. You're going to see some tremendous and wonderful things happen in your life because of your sacrifice.

A Spiritual Powerline to say out loud:
"I WALK IN MY ANOINTING!"

A powerful prayer to pray:
Lord, I am encouraged today. I know that You have anointed me to receive and achieve all that You have planned for my life. While I wait, please strengthen me. Help me stay on the altar of sacrifice until I see everything fulfilled You have put in my heart. I believe You will take care of me and meet my needs during this time. In the name of Jesus. Amen.

NOTES:

_____

_____

_____

Day 70

You're Going to Something Much Better

There are times we can feel that we're in a desert. Things have dried up. Our needs and desires are not being fulfilled. We're not flourishing in some area of our life.

This is where Moses was. He had left Egypt because he had lost favor with Pharaoh, and he ended up on a desert in Midian. There he received a job tending sheep for the man who eventually became his father-in-law.

So there Moses was. On the backside of the desert tending sheep. He started out being the adopted son of the daughter of Pharaoh of Egypt—the most powerful man in the world at that time.

He was raised in wealth and knowledge. Trained to be a prince. Had a promise of power and ease. He had it good.

You know how it is when things are going good. We feel as though we're on top. No major trials. We're just going alooong in life. Then boom. Something goes wrong. Before we know it, we're dealing with concerns, worries, and problems. We feel we're on the backside of the desert and all the things that make us happy are not making us happy anymore. We feel disappointed. Dissatisfied. Maybe even a little desperate.

I imagine Moses was dealing with those types of feelings. How many times did he replay the way things had gone for him and wondered over and over what the future was going to be. How many times does your mind run on the events of what is happening to you and you wonder what the future holds? **You're in a desert experience. But that's where you can grow in God and come out of it a better person—greater in who you are and what you can do!**

Oh yes, when you grow through those experiences, you come out of them more powerful, with greater faith and ability. You see a higher level of answers and miracles. There is much to gain by allowing yourself to grow in the midst of tough circumstances. Even though it seems as if you're at a stepping-down point, as you have faith in God, you are stepping up to what He has for you.

Remember that—when it seems as though you're stepping down, you're stepping up...to what God has for you. Believe for your desert experience to turn into an experience of becoming closer to God and entering into a new season of blessing and accomplishment.

In the desert is where Moses had his first great encounter with God. He turned aside to see the burning bush and God spoke to him. He gave him a new life. Because Moses had been in the desert and acquired knowledge of the area and had learned how to take care of sheep, he was now prepared to lead millions of God's sheep through the same desert he had been in as he delivered the Israelites from Egyptian bondage!

You may be in a desert experience, but as you turn to God in faith here's what will happen:

You will gain spiritual depth that will better equip you for the future.

You'll be able to see miracles that before seemed impossible.

You will reach fulfillment and a power level beyond what you dreamed.

So keep all this in mind as the desert days get long and tough and know that you're going to something better. Much better! You're growing into it. You'll come out of the desert with the power and blessing of God on you.

A Spiritual Powerline to say out loud:
"I'M GOING TO SOMETHING MUCH BETTER!"

A powerful prayer to pray:
Lord, I feel that I'm in a desert experience, but I know You're here with me. You're growing me and taking me to something much better. I'm not stepping down, but I'm stepping up to what You have for me. Strengthen me during the desert days so I can encounter You in a greater way and gain all that is waiting for me. In the name of Jesus. Amen.

NOTES:

_____

_____

_____

Day 71

When You Endure...

Sometimes when we're going through a nighttime type of experience we may wonder, *Oh, will I ever get out of this?* We know the scripture says that weeping endures for a night, but joy comes in the morning (Psalm 30:5). Well, we've had plenty of weeping, but where's the joy? That's when our endurance is being tested.

When Daniel was thrown into the lions' den by the king because he refused to stop praying to his God, he had to endure a nighttime experience. Now when you're in the pit and lions are in there with you and they're hungry, the key to survival is to endure the night without teeth marks or claw marks. Survive. Endure. That's what the faith of Daniel enabled him to do. He knew Someone greater was with him than what was surrounding him.

That's the picture God wants you to have right now for your life. In the pit of the problem is Someone with you Who is greater than what you're facing. Just as sure as He covered Daniel from those lions, He is covering you.

In the morning, the king rushed to the den and cried out to Daniel to see if he was still in one piece. Daniel called back to him, "My God has sent His Angel and has shut the mouths of the lions so they have not hurt me" (Daniel 6:22). Then the king brought Daniel out and promoted him.

Remember this: **when you endure the night with the lions, you will be promoted in the morning by the King.** Endure that nighttime experience and then experience all the good God has planned for you. Your answer. Your desire. The lion, the devil, who roams about trying to devour you, cannot eat up your desires and dreams—if you endure. God will shut his mouth. By faith, when you endure the night in the pit, you're promoted in the morning by the King!

A Spiritual Powerline to say out loud:
"I ENDURE FOR THE PROMOTION!"

A powerful prayer to pray:
Lord, I am in a nighttime experience right now. But I know You are here with me. And You are greater than the circumstances. I pray You give me faith and strength to endure. The weeping is over and joy is coming! I'm going from the pit to promotion—into the answers and desires You have for me. I praise You for this. In the name of Jesus. Amen.

NOTES:

_____

_____

_____

Day 72
_____

Watch for the Signal

In Proverbs Chapter 3, we're told that if we trust in God with all our heart and mind and we don't rely on our own understanding and insight, He will direct us.

So if we want direction, it's a matter of trust. To trust and rely on Him means we wait for His signal! He will indicate when it's the right time to move and where we move. He's the One who can see down the path, so He knows what's going to happen and the repercussions.

But sometimes we get antsy waiting for His signal. Maybe we missed it? Or perhaps we should go ahead because God isn't going to send a sign. Then if we move ahead, that's when we feel the repercussions.

A good way to view this is how a professional baseball player learned the importance of waiting for the signal from his baseball manager. The manager had a rule that no one could steal a base until they were given the steal sign. But this player felt he could judge when he could steal, based on what he knew about who was pitching and who was catching. So one game he decided he was going to do it. He watched the pitcher, got a good jump on him and made it to second base before the ball could get him out. He was happy! He had shown the manager how he had the ability to make the judgment call.

Whenever we get to the place we think we can make the right judgment call without relying on God, that's when we can create some tough conditions for ourselves. That's when the dominoes begin to fall because we didn't see the repercussions that could come.

So, after the game, the manager took the player aside and began to show him the reason that he should not steal without receiving a signal. Even though he thought it worked out great, he could not see the whole picture. Here's what happened because this player stole base. First, the very next batter was one of their best power hitters. When this player stole second base that meant first base became open. So when the power hitter came to bat, the opposing team was able to walk him to first base. Had the player stayed on first base, the batter could have possibly gotten a good hit and both of them would have made it home.

The second problem that resulted was that the third batter was not strong against the opposing pitcher. So that meant the manager had to send up a pinch-hitter to try to get the two players on first and second base home. Because he had to do that, that meant he did not have strong players on the bench for later in the game when he must have them.

The Lord sees the bigger picture and even though we think it's okay to move ahead, He knows why it isn't. **There's going to be better results if we wait for the signal.** And that's what we want after all—the best results. We want a home run. There are just some moments in our life when we should not move out. Don't move. If we do, we go right past the best of what God has. When we adhere to the spiritual stop signs, that's when we eventually end up in the right way and we receive what will fulfill our heart and give us great joy and satisfaction. We can see tremendous miracles done that way.

Trust that God will point you in the right direction. The signal will be obvious. It will be so obvious that if you are trusting in Him and confident in what He will do, you will be at peace. God will show you the right way to take for a breakthrough. His directions will be apparent.

Think how the children of Israel waited for God's signal before they went in to take over the city of Jericho. Joshua Chapter 6 describes how God gave them instructions that when they heard the sound of the trumpet, all the people should set out, and that's when the wall around the city would fall in its place and they could go up into it and fight for God.

It happened just as God promised because they did it His way. There was a loud blast of the trumpet. The signal was given! All the people shouted with a great shout. Then the wall of the enclosure fell down in its place and the army went up into the city and took it. They had a home run victory over that place and now they could receive the blessing of the land of promise.

Get ready to hear a trumpet blast to give the signal! God is sending you in for a victory. Wait for the sign. Even if you feel antsy at times, establish in yourself that you will listen and watch for it. Rest inside that you will know just what to do. And as you take His directions, you will have a home run.

A Spiritual Powerline to say out loud:
"I'M WAITING FOR THE VICTORY SIGNAL!"

A powerful prayer to pray:
Lord, I trust in You with all my heart and mind. I will not rely on my own insight or ability. You direct my path into victory. So, I have a home run. I'm going into the place You have promised me. In the name of Jesus. Amen.

NOTES:

_____

_____

_____

Day 73

He Shall Bring It Forth

God knows the longing that's in your heart, what you want to see fulfilled, and the hopes that are deep within you. But at the present, those hopes may not seem as if they will ever come to pass. You've wanted something so much, but time goes on and you still don't see it. You need something special to happen from God. **That's when He shows up to give birth to those hopes.**

That's how it happened for Abraham and Sarah. They had waited a long time to have a child. Now they were getting too old to have one. Yet, they held onto the promise which God had given them, just as you're holding onto the promise He's given you to meet your needs and fulfill what He's put in your heart.

It was deep in Sarah's heart to have a child and family. And because she held to that with her faith, Genesis 21 says, *The Lord visited Sarah as He had said, and the Lord did for her as He had promised. For Sarah became pregnant and bore Abraham a son in his old age, at the set time God had told him* (Genesis 21:1, 2).

The hopes were there. The faith was in her heart. She was standing on the Word of God. And so it was the Lord made a visit to Sarah just as He had said. He came to give birth to their hopes.

Let me tell you, the Lord is about to make a visit to you just as He has said. He will come to give birth to your hopes. Hold them close to your heart. Keep faith in you. Stand on the Word of God.

It's time for you to see what the Lord has for you. In Isaiah 66 He poses this question to you: *Shall I bring to the moment of birth and not cause to bring forth? says the Lord. Shall I Who causes to bring forth shut the womb? says your God.*

He has placed hopes in your heart, and He's brought them to the moment of birth. Now would He not cause them to come forth? He's asking a rhetorical question. "Shall I Who causes to bring forth shut the womb?" In other words, "Shall I cause your hopes to come forth and then shut off the birth before it takes place and abort it?" Oh no, God will not do that. He's not going to shut down your hopes and have you be deserted and disappointed. **He is showing how obvious it is that you can believe for Him to give birth to what He's placed in your heart. Since He is the One who did it, He will be the One to fulfill it.**

For instance, if you've been ill or in pain, God has put hope in your heart that you can be well. And when you pray and believe and express faith, you're preparing yourself for the answer to come. But when doubt or fear or discouragement tries to come, that's when you have to remember Isaiah 66. Remember that He's showing how crazy it would be for Him to give birth to your hopes to be well and not cause them to come forth. He's not going to shut off the very avenue of your being able to become well. He shall bring it forth. He wants to give birth to your hopes. Believe for them to come into existence and for your body or emotions or mind to be made whole.

Now appropriate this same concept to every part of your life that needs a visit from God. He's ready to bring it about. He's ready to cause it to come to pass in those special circumstances you're facing. The job challenge. The business decrease. You can have a visit from God in your marriage. Oh just think of God coming into your home and doing a great work. In those relationships that are causing you consternation, God can be there.

He's there when you're facing a bad report or a legal entanglement. He visits you in the night when you're in sorrow or grief. Reach out for your Lord when anxiety or worry is trying to fill you. Ask Him to visit your children and grandchildren. To visit your church and ministry. Yes, God sees this thing that you're trying to complete, and He is there to enable you to do it.

Allow Him to give birth to your hopes and see them fulfilled. Prepare your heart in faith that He will do this. Be watching. Listen for Him.

Praise God, I can just feel this coming forth in the Spirit! The Lord your God is making Himself known to you. He sees what's in your heart and the need you have. It's now time for Him to give birth to those hopes. Believe today that God is saying, "I shall bring it forth!"

A Spiritual Powerline to say out loud:
"GOD WILL BRING IT FORTH!"

A powerful prayer to pray:
Lord, my heart is filled with the hopes that You placed there. You gave birth to them. So now, I believe You will bring them forth. I'm expecting something big, beautiful, and powerful to happen. In the name of Jesus. Amen.

Jeanne Alcott

NOTES:

_____

_____

_____

Day 74

Can It Change?

Have you ever wondered if something could change? *Will I continue to deal with this forever?*

It's during those times that we want to show God we believe He CAN change conditions. We expect! We're determined to keep praying and believing until it happens...even though we don't see what He is doing.

There's an inspiring story of how an older woman did this for her church. It shows what can happen when we *stay on the watch* and don't give up believing God is working for us. This happened in a church in East Texas when a minister had been invited to hold a series of meetings at the church.

From the beginning, it was obvious to everyone that something very special was happening. It was as if people from all over the place were coming to the church. Those who had stopped going and turned from God came to the services and turned back to serving Him. People were receiving the baptism of the Holy Spirit. Others were finding a new depth in God they had never experienced. Lives were being transformed. It was an amazing change in the church that was beyond what most people had expected could possibly happen.

184

While the pastor was excited, he could not understand why all of a sudden this breakthrough would come to the church. So one day as he was questioning the Lord about it, the Holy Spirit prompted him to think of a woman who had been going to the church for quite some time. She was a very quiet type person. The pastor knew God must have brought her to his mind for a reason. So he could barely wait until the service that night to talk with her.

After service, he made his way to her and began to explain what had happened when he was praying that morning and how God had brought her to his mind in relation to what was occurring in the church now. So he asked her if she knew what it was all about. That's when she broke down and started to cry.

You see, for over a year she had been doing what God had led her to do. She had written down the names of every person who had visited the church. Then during the week she would take the names of those people and pray over them. She was consistent and determined to obey God. Even though nothing evident was happening each week as she would pray over these people, she knew God was working. She was just waiting for the change to come. It took over a year, but God sent His Spirit to that church in a revival that has been the greatest ever to happen in that area.

That woman didn't **leave the watch**. She continued to pray and watch for what God would send. Something was going on that whole year even though she couldn't see it. And something is going on right now with you. What you've been talking to God about and praying for—something is happening. Don't think it's not going anywhere. **God is initiating the plans. He's going into action.** Just keep thinking about how you will see the results of what He's been doing just as that woman saw it in her church.

I know it's hard to believe when we see nothing—no action. But remember, we are dealing in the natural realm—God deals in the supernatural realm. And there's plenty of activity going on in the supernatural realm. He is working, but so is the devil.

So here is what happens when you are expecting there to be a change. God looks past the enemy and his efforts and He sees you. He observes how you are watching. You're waiting and expecting. **Instead of turning away and believing that change can never happen, you are attentive and hopeful. It's in your voice and in your eyes and in your spirit.** You know God is working even though you can't see it and so you keep watching with faith. And God responds to that!

He pushes the devil aside and sends His answer right past him. Your answer bursts through the spiritual realm and into the natural realm right where you are.

Can your situation change? Just watch!

A Spiritual Powerline to say out loud:
"CHANGE IS HAPPENING!"

A powerful prayer to pray:
Oh Lord, I believe You can bring change into my conditions. So I'm expecting. See expectation in my eyes and in my spirit and hear it in my voice. I believe my Lord will send the miracle answer even though I don't see You working now. So I'm on the watch! It's coming. In the name of Jesus. Amen.

NOTES:

_____

_____

_____

Day 75

Don't Settle for Joyless Drudgery

Do you feel at times that you don't have an enjoyable life? We know that's not how God intends it to be, but we may feel that we are experiencing joyless drudgery.

That's when we have to keep our eyes on the Lord and why we're doing what we're doing. Why are you enduring? Why are you persevering? For what reason do you keep going? What's your desire? Your goal? Remember the "why." Instead of enduring each day and not enjoying it because of difficulties or disappointments, remember why you are working and praying and believing.

If you lose sight of that, then your life and even your love for others can become *a have-to* instead of a choice. You feel, *I have to do this.* But you can change that to, *I want to do this so I can see God's will done. I want to fulfill His desires for me. I can have a wonderful life.*

Now what can you do on those days when it seems too hard to get there? You don't feel it. On those days, pray for the Holy Spirit to motivate you. Sometimes you need extra help. So pray, "Holy Spirit, motivate me today. I'm having problems to keep going. Remind me of why I'm doing this and energize my spirit and heart to go on. I want to experience my wonderful life."

And the Holy Spirit will be spot-on. He will cause your thoughts and emotions to line up with what God wants to do for you. The Holy Spirit knows what's waiting just around the corner for you, and He is there to strengthen and help you get on around that corner and not stop short until you experience the great blessing God has.

This is what a woman did when she had a sudden change in her life. She was thirty-seven years old when her husband suddenly died of a heart attack. So she became a widow with three children. The burden became so heavy she said she felt forsaken and that her life was not worth living anymore. Working. Raising those children. Helping them when they went through rebellious stages of life. Making ends meet. No enjoyment in life.

That's when she turned to God and in the midst of what she was experiencing, the Holy Spirit gave her strength and courage and took her out of joyless drudgery. She kept before her why she was doing all she had to do. Now here is what she says, "I look back on all of it, and I can see three beautiful children, happily married, raising their children in church. And I know that through it all, God never let me down!"

In spite of how things appear, remember there is a reason why you keep going. **And as you set your sights on the "why," it can lighten your spirit. Make your days more hopeful. Cause you to rest inside and actually have enjoyment. Things won't seem so hard for you then.**

How many times have you set your mind on what you desire, and even though the times were difficult to receive it, happiness came into you each time you thought of what God was doing and where He was taking you? That's the enjoyment God wants you to feel as you keep your mind on what is coming.

Think how this happened in the life of Jacob in the Bible. He wanted to marry beautiful Rachel, the daughter of his Uncle Laban. But her father determined that Jacob should work for him seven years before he would give Rachel to him. Nevertheless, as Jacob worked over the years, it was not joyless drudgery for him. Every time Rachel walked by him and smiled as he worked, he remembered why he was doing it! So Genesis 29:20 says, *And Jacob served seven years for Rachel; and they seemed to him but a few days because of the love he had for her.*

Do you believe God can do that for you? That He can take the days when you are dealing with waiting for something, desiring it, working for it, and He can still make those days be wonderful? If you believe that and you ask Him for it, you will receive.

He can send events and experiences and blessings to you to help you each day until you see the "why" fulfilled. Because you know why you're doing what you're doing and having faith, you will come to the point that you can thank God for a wonderful life.

A Spiritual Powerline to say out loud:
"I ENJOY MY LIFE!"

A powerful prayer to pray:
Lord, You know the days when it's tough for me to enjoy life. So, I pray Your Holy Spirit motivate and strengthen me to go on. I receive the enjoyment and great blessings You have waiting for me just around the corner. In the name of Jesus. Amen.

NOTES:

_____

_____

_____

Day 76

No Human or Hell Can Stop It

Have you ever gone on a mission trip? Many Christians have, but back in the early 1700s not only did Christians usually not go on missions but full-time missionaries were virtually nonexistent in some parts of the world.

In 1732, Leonard Dober and David Nitschmann were commissioned to the West Indies to bring a breakthrough and establish missions work. Their hearts were inspired and excited.

But when they landed in Monrovia on their way to Copenhagen, there was one obstacle after another. Then some opposition in the area came out against the mission. Leonard and David couldn't even find a ship that would take them to the West Indies.

One morning when they opened their devotional book for the day, God spoke to their discouraged hearts through the scripture in Numbers 23:19, *Has God said, and will He not do it? Or has He spoken, and will He not make it good?*

Hasn't He told you that He would do this? Hasn't He assured you time and again that you are going to see your desire completed? Believe He will make His Word good! Human or hell cannot stop it.

These two missionaries had faith in that scripture and that's when they got a breakthrough. Things began to turn. A handful of people in Copenhagen began to have favor on them. Then two chaplains from the royal court of Denmark supported them. They told Princess Charlotte about the missionaries and she gave a good amount of donations to help with their expenses. Finally, they found a Dutch ship that would take them to the West Indies where they did a great work and opened the modern era of missions.

When circumstances are discouraging, believe that human or hell cannot stop what God will do. He will make it good as you have faith.

A Spiritual Powerline to say out loud:
"GOD WILL MAKE IT GOOD!"

A powerful prayer to pray:
Lord, it seems as though everything is trying to stop Your answer from coming to me. But I believe You will fulfill the desire You placed in my heart. No human or hell can stop what You are doing. You will make it good! I praise You for this. In the name of Jesus. Amen.

NOTES:

_____

_____

_____

Day 77
_____

Replace Hurt With Hope

God wants to talk to you about the dreams that have been broken or stolen or forgotten. Those hopes and desires that almost seem dead now. He will breathe energy and hope into them. He's going to take you to the top of the mountain spiritually and show you a vision of how hardships and disappointments cannot stop your dreams.

That's because in spite of what is against your dreams, God is for them. So when something tries to make them seem impossible, God ignores the impossible. You have to ignore the impossible also. That will enable you to continue hoping for what God puts in your heart.

A woman describes how she had to come to this place in her life concerning her desire to be married. She was in her thirties and she had experienced one disappointment after another. So much so that she said, "Holding onto the hope that marriage was still possible and that God would provide a husband did not come easily." So to counteract that, and get past the disappointments, she adopted being cynical. She felt doing this protected her heart and her mind from hurting over what she could not have. She was very sarcastic about ever being married.

But eventually she said that didn't work either. She still had the pain in her heart and she also knew that being cynical would not cause the man God intended for her to be attracted to her. She needed the Lord to restore her dream.

That's when she made a conscious decision to fight for hope. She knew it wouldn't be easy, but she prayed for God to give her strength. It worked. Today she is a newlywed. Her dream has been fulfilled to be married and have a family.

That may never have happened if she had not said "no" to the word impossible and allowed God to heal the hurt and pain in her heart. **The hurt had to be replaced with hope.** That in turn helped her get over the disappointments so she could once again believe God's will would be done in her life. He had put that desire in her, and He would fulfill it. So when she came to the place that she could ignore the impossible and embrace the possibility of what God could do, that's when she saw the dream completed.

We can start getting the feeling, *Is this ever going to happen?* And that's when the impossible starts growing so much larger than what was possible to us at one time. So we have to come to a decisive moment as this woman did. We're not going to get into an attitude or into wrong thinking in order to protect our heart from pain and disappointment. But we're going to ask God to protect us and then to restore our dream and strengthen us to remain hopeful.

As we walk in that faith, that's what will attract the dream. Now really envision this. **If you're a person full of hope and belief that God will fulfill the dreams He placed in you, then you're attracting the dream to come and be fulfilled.**

You believe in what God believes in—the completion of what He has for you.

So you are ignoring what God ignores—the impossible.

And you embrace what He embraces—the dream becoming possible.

You refuse to be sold a bill of goods that the vision within you cannot come to pass.

Oh yes, the Lord is restoring your dreams as you are filled with the belief that they are possible. You walk hand-in-hand with God by your faith—walking into the completion of your dream. What seemed impossible at one time will fall to the side and you can laugh at it because you're now living out your dream.

God can send new strength and energy into you so you have new hope. He will restore your dreams and that's when you can see them come to pass.

A Spiritual Powerline to say out loud:
"MY DREAMS COME TO PASS!"

A powerful prayer to pray:
Lord, I'm ready for my dreams to be fulfilled! So I ignore the impossible. I laugh at it. And I believe You make all things possible. I shall live in the visions, hopes, and desires You've put in my heart. In the name of Jesus. Amen.

NOTES:

_____

_____

_____

Day 78

It's Worth Your Wait

Have you asked God for something and you can't figure out why there is such a delay in getting your answer? Here is something you can remember during this time that will encourage you: God can make it worth your wait.

Let me show you what's going on behind the scenes when you are waiting, even when you don't realize it.

There's a woman who went to a farmer's market with which she was familiar and had gone there often. It happened to be in the afternoon and it was hot as she stood in a long line. But she wanted to buy some grapes so she decided to wait. As she did, she noticed how the owner was being kind and attentive to each person.

Then when she finally got to the front of the line and gave her order for the grapes she wanted, the owner just said, "Please excuse me for a minute." Then he disappeared! He walked away. Right away she felt this was so rude and unfair. Everyone else had been served immediately and received the product they wanted, and she had been waiting patiently in the heat, and now here she was told to wait some more. And he didn't even take time to tell her why.

She didn't appreciate being forced to wait this way. So she began to get angry. Perturbed. By the time the owner reappeared, she was *not* happy. The way we can get sometimes when we are waiting and we don't know why.

When the owner returned, she noticed he had a big smile on his face as he walked up to the table, and in his hands were some of the biggest and best grapes she had ever seen. Then he offered for her to taste test them, so she took one of them and ate it. As soon as she did, she could tell they were some of the best she had ever tasted. So right away she purchased them and was ready to rush off when the owner said to her, "I'm sure sorry you had to wait, but I wanted to make sure that I gave you my very best." He had made it worth her wait. She had received the biggest, best, and most delicious grapes of all.

You know, we can always get something faster, but it may not turn out to be the best. If we surrender to wait for God's timing, then it will be worth it. The "grapes" will be the biggest. The best.

We're being asked to wait because God wants to give us His best.

The Lord is teaching us something through the whole process. He's growing us. He's actually growing our faith, **because to wait and do it the right way means that your faith has to grow stronger.** Then what happens when your faith grows? You're able to believe for more!

It's amazing how He did this for Abraham and Sarah. When their names were still Abram and Sarai, God brought Abram outside his tent into the starlight and told him to turn his face toward the heavens. Then He said to him, *Fear not, Abram, I am your Shield, your abundant compensation, and your reward shall be exceedingly great* (Genesis 15:1). That's when Abram spoke up and said in essence, "That's great, God. But what can You give me since I don't even have a child to inherit it?"

See, he had been waiting such a long time for a child that now it seemed it was not possible. That's when the Father told Abram to look at the stars. Why the stars? Because they were the only thing numerous enough that could demonstrate to Abram how big his blessing was going to be. "Look at the stars, Abram!" He was going to give him a son, Isaac, and from him would come generations who would serve God and be Abram's descendants. Oh, God made it worth his wait.

This blessing was so wonderful that it called for a name change. No more would he be known as Abram, which meant "exalted father," but God changed his name to Abraham which means "father of a multitude!" Exceedingly fruitful. And Sarai's name became Sarah which means "Princess." Their reward for waiting would be exceedingly great just as God had said.

The Lord makes it worth your wait. Get ready for Him to change your name. You will go from being called *Dissatisfied* to *Pleased*. From *Frustrated* to *Fulfilled*. You are waiting for the name change so you can possess all God has for you. So don't get discouraged as you're waiting in line.

You just keep hanging on, because when God does it, He's going to do it big. He will do it right. Let Him determine how much and when you receive your blessing. It's worth the wait.

A Spiritual Powerline to say out loud:
"I WAIT FOR THE BEST!"

A powerful prayer to pray:
Dear God, I believe You are working on something great for me. Even though I'm tired of waiting, I know it will be worth it. You're doing what is best for my life. So I'm excited about the name change You're giving me. I will not be called Disappointed, but I am called Delighted! Thank You for what is coming by Your hand. In the name of Jesus. Amen.

NOTES:

_____

_____

_____

Day 79

It Will Come...Eventually

You know how it is to want something sooo much! You want it right away—and you want ALL of it. The whole answer. The entire blessing. The complete change to take place.

But most of us have been there where we didn't see it ALL happen at once. There was a beginning, then progress, and then eventually we had what we desired and all of it. So during those times when we have to stand in faith for something, we need to reassure ourselves with this truth—it may come a portion at a time! Piece by piece!

The key is the victory will come eventually. That's what counts— it WILL be done. It just may come piece by piece according to God's wisdom and His will.

This is what the Israelites had to believe for God to do. When it came time for them to take ownership of the property that God had promised them, they didn't get all of it at one time. They would go into an area and the Lord would instruct them when it was the right timing to defeat the enemies that were in that area. Then when they followed Him, they would have a conquest and take over that portion of land. In fact, with Joshua leading them it took seven years to complete all of their victories.

They knew it would not come into their possession all at once because in Exodus 23:30, God had told the people, *Little by little I will drive [the enemies] out from before you, until you have increased and are numerous enough to take possession of the land.*

He said that He would not drive them out in just one year. If He did, the land would become desolate because they could not take care of the ground and cause it to be fruitful. The weeds would grow up and the wild animals would multiply and actually harm the people. It would become a place of hardship and danger.

That's where you are. **You are just about to take ownership of the property God has promised**—your health, financial well-being, a position, you're just about to come to the place in that relationship where you get married or have a better marriage, or a better relationship with your children or someone important to you. You're about to take ownership of conditions at your work becoming better or your home or your country. That new position you desire. The legal suit. Think of something in your life now that you can tell you're about to take ownership of it. But it is coming piece by piece.

197

Yet, the whole time God is driving the enemy out before you just as He drove those inhabitants out of the land the Israelites were about take over. But He did it piece by piece so there would be time for the people to increase in number and ability. Otherwise the weeds and wild animals would have taken over and devoured them.

So God knows what He's doing—it's His wisdom and His will. And it's going to come to you a portion at a time so you have time to be able to handle what's coming. You're smart enough to know that you don't want it before God's timing because you'll have to deal with the problems and the damaging repercussions. **So instead of the weeds and wild animals, you want God's wisdom and His will.**

God knows how fast to give you the answers and the victories. So sometimes He will give you a portion of the answer at a time. But never doubt you *will* receive what He has for you in its entirety as you have faith to continue on. Believe it will come...eventually.

A Spiritual Powerline to say out loud:
"IT WILL COME!"

A powerful prayer to pray:
Lord, I desire Your wisdom and Your will in my life. So I put my situation in Your hands. I know You will help me take ownership of the victory that is mine. It's coming and I receive it by faith. In the name of Jesus. Amen.

NOTES:

_____

_____

_____

Day 80

You Will Arrive at the Best Place

When you have faith for God to do something, His power cannot be stopped. When the stormy circumstances are raging, believe they cannot impede what God is going to do for you. You will arrive at the best place when it's all over.

There's an amazing story of how a group of people experienced this concerning their church building. The church was in North Carolina near the ocean, and it turned out that it was a bad place to be, especially when a hurricane hit one day.

After it subsided, they viewed the damage to the church building, then got busy and restored everything in it. Unfortunately, a short time after the first hurricane, another one struck. Once more, the members got together and repaired everything. However, this time they decided it would be good to find a new location—one that would be safer.

So, after they had scouted out some locations, they found the perfect property that would be safe and they could afford. A good offer was made to the owner of the property, however, he didn't want to sell.

While they were still negotiating with him, another hurricane came to that area. This was the third one! It created a tremendous flood in the town and the waters were so strong, they literally raised the church building off its moorings and floated it downstream.

It was an amazing scene to watch as people tried everything, even tying ropes to the building, to try to prevent it from floating further away. Nothing worked.

How discouraging. They've had multiple storms hit the church. Repairs have had to be done twice on the church. They have tried to find a safer place. And the one piece of property they want won't be sold to them by the man who owns it. Now another storm has come and the church is floating down the streets of the town!

When the storms have hit against you, they have picked you up and tried to push you out of what God has for you, keep your faith. Know that God is moving in your behalf. He will make sure that His will is done. **Those storms cannot hold back His power working for you. He will get you to the place you desire.**

The next morning the church people got up and began to try to find where their church had landed. Where was it? Smack dab on the piece of ground which they had tried to purchase. There it was. Right on the spot. So, they went to the owner and made their offer again to purchase the land.

He said that he would not take their money for the property. But then he added, "I'll give it to you. The Lord definitely wants this church on this ground."

Not only did they get the place they desired, but they received a blessing on top of that—it was free! God used the very thing that came against them to accomplish His will.

It may seem as though the storm, the circumstances, the difficulty and problems and pain are in control. They are pushing your life along. Yet, they are so small compared to what God can do. He can use the very thing that is coming against you to accomplish His will. Your thoughts and emotions and beliefs will not be torn by the storm, but you actually will become stronger and arrive at a better place.

Right this moment, as God's Spirit is touching your heart, believe that He is doing something. He already has made the plan, and He has started the action. He will not be held back by any storm! No matter how severe. No matter how problematic that storm is, it cannot change what God will do. He sees the faith in your heart in the face of what is raging. Now, He's releasing the plan He has for you.

Just as that church, **you will arrive at the best place and be blessed on top of it.**

Isaiah 54:14, 15: *You shall establish yourself in...conformity with God's will. Whoever stirs up strife against you shall fall and surrender to you.*

A Spiritual Powerline to say out loud:
"I ARRIVE AT THE BEST PLACE AND BLESSED!"

A powerful prayer to pray:
Lord, I know this storm coming against me is not stronger than Your power. It will not be able to push me out of Your will. I'm going to come out of this and not just that, but I'm coming out of it with blessing! In the name of Jesus. Amen.

NOTES:

_____

_____

_____

Day 81

When Your Plans Are Upset

A man was overseas, trying to get home when there was a layover in a small Amazonian airport. He was not happy! He had been on two flights already and wanted to get to his room and rest. Now here he was in an uncomfortable chair in a hot and stuffy airport.

So he got up and began to stomp around the airport, sighing and showing his exasperation. Then he noticed there was a monk in the airport who was supposed be on the same flight as he was. However, he was facing the delay in a different way. This monk found an empty chair, got as comfortable as he could, and began to nod off. Well, that frustrated this man even more. He thought, *While I am stewing, this guy is snoring.*

So after the monk awoke, the man said something to him about it, and here is how he replied to him, "What else could I do? God is in control." This man was a Christian so he knew what the monk had said was true—God is in control. Instead of getting bent out of shape, being concerned about his plans and what was happening, he could have rested in God.

I can just see myself there, can you? The times I have stomped around, at least in my emotions if not physically. Impatient. Upset that my plans were spoiled. That's when we need to stop and ask ourselves if we are trying to walk out of God's plans without realizing it. After all, they are not supposed to be *our* plans. All that matters is if we are in the flow of what God is doing and where He is taking us. And if there seems to be an interruption, that's not going to stop the flow of what God can do. Nothing can stop Him when we trust.

So we must decide to be patient and rest in Him. That's when we begin to see things through God's eyes. Our spirit takes over and gives us greater understanding and ability to make it through every circumstance.

Psalm 37 tells us to rest in the Lord, wait for Him, and patiently lean ourselves upon Him. Cease from anger and don't fret (Psalm 37:7, 8). Now just get that picture! This is not the picture of a frustrated, upset type of person—but it's describing one who faces life with confidence and assurance. This person knows their God is good, and He is more powerful than anything that happens to them. They're not going to get into anger or fret and worry. They rest in God and wait for Him to act.

That's the picture of us. We're not going to run around with worry. **We're not going to be upset when our plans are upset.** But we cease from that. We tell anger to get away and worry and stress to be gone. We are waiting on God because we know He's got the true answer we need. So we're leaning on Him. No matter what happens we know He will come through and work out everything for our good. We are in a state of rest. **That opens the door for God to take control and fulfill His plan for us.**

We can be as the monk. Find a chair. Get as comfortable as possible. And know that God is in control. Instead of being frustrated or impatient and then worn-out because we've been spiritually stomping all over the place, we will be refreshed and ready to go into all God has for us. We can rest in that. We can rest in God.

A Spiritual Powerline to say out loud:
"I'M IN GOD'S PLANS!"

A powerful prayer to pray:
Lord, I believe I am in Your plans and You're in control. Help me to rest in You when things are frustrating. As I do, I believe You are changing conditions. Now, I walk into all the good that You have planned. In the name of Jesus. Amen.

NOTES:

_____

_____

_____

Day 82

God Will Be There

In the moment when you need Him, God will be there. Allow Him to demonstrate what He can do. Prove Him.

Sean and Nikki came to a place in their lives in which they had to trust that God would be there for them. This couple had always given to God's work, because they felt it created a covering for their life according to Malachi 3:10, 11. That scripture promises that God will pour out blessings from heaven and rebuke the devourer that comes against us. He will cause our efforts to be productive, and we can see things accomplished.

The time came when Sean and Nikki had to prove that promise from God. The first thing that happened was that Sean's company started cutting back his hours. But in all the months that his salary was cut, they said it was supernatural. Their bills were paid and their account never went below $1000. Now, you have to know that their account was never that high even when Sean was working full time. But now it stayed at $1000 after all the bills were paid. Never ran out. They couldn't explain how.

What does that remind you of? Think about the widow and the prophet Elijah during the famine in I Kings 17. Elijah asked her to sustain him by giving him a portion of the last meal and oil that she had. She had just enough food to cook one more meal and then she and her son were going to die in the famine. But because she stepped out and gave to the Lord by supplying this prophet with food and drink, she proved that God was mightier than famine, need, or fear.

The Bible says that her meal and oil never were depleted during the entire economic difficulty—just as Sean's and Nikki's account never was depleted. They were the financial meal and oil to sustain them.

Then of course the enemy struck again as he always does. The next blow came when Sean's company announced it would close down in two years. He began a job search and although he tried, he could not find one. Over a year went by and they were running out of time. Then they got down to two months before the company was closing. It was time to prove God. So they did just what His Word prescribes. They continued giving to God, praying, and trusting Him.

Two months before the closing date of Sean's company, he received his new job. On top of that, his new boss allowed him to complete his contract with the current company so he could receive a great severance package when he left.

The devil was trying to drain and steal their well-being, their family, and their provision. But because they trusted God and obeyed His Word they showed what He could do for those who believe Him. Don't you know He had fun demonstrating His power and compassion for them? God wants us to prove Him.

Step out and trust for the area where you need the Lord to do something. When you step out and trust, He confirms your trust. He can create time, health, restoration, fulfillment, and accomplishment. What do you need? Prove Him. That's what He invites you to do in His Word...no, He *compels* you to do it. The Lord knows you cannot reach your full potential without doing this. You have to have Him. And He will be there when you need Him.

You can trust Him to come through. Believe that for every area of your life at this moment. He wants to show you that He's powerful and good. Now is the time for you to prove God!

A Spiritual Powerline to say out loud:
"GOD IS HERE FOR ME!"

A powerful prayer to pray:
God, I'm stepping out today and trusting You. As I do, I know You are here for me. Now, I'm ready for You to demonstrate Your power and compassion. I accept Your command to prove You. And I trust You to come through. In the name of Jesus. Amen.

NOTES:

_____

_____

_____

Day 83

Step by Step

There's a poem that says,
God does not lead me year by year
Nor even day by day,
But step by step my path unfolds;
My Lord directs my way.
The God who gave His Son
Holds all my moments in His hand
And gives them, one by one.

God does not usually show you everything at once concerning the direction you are to take or the answer you need, but as you rely on Him, you will see what to do...next. God unfolds your path step by step.

Now that can be hard when you are lying in bed at night wondering about things. *How in the world is this ever going to come together? When will I know what to do? I'm running out of time. I've been trying to find a way to conquer this but I just don't know which direction to take.*

All those thousand and one things that come up where you simply need direction. It's almost as if the answer is hidden. You need God to shine some light on the path so you can see what to do, where to go.

So what does God's Word say to you when you are in this kind of situation? He promises in Psalm 97:11, *Light is sown for the uncompromisingly righteous and spread along their pathway.*

So here's how it works: God throws light down onto your path and you can see where to take one step. Once you take a step, then there will be light for the next step. Take it. That's what faith is all about. Just step by step. He will give you light as you need it.

That's what a man discovered when he came to the place where he couldn't find the direction to take for an invention on which he was working. Samuel Morse had established himself as a successful painter and was commissioned to paint a portrait of Lafayette in Washington DC in 1825. While there, he received a note from a messenger on horseback that his wife was not feeling well. Before he could get home to Connecticut to her, he received another message that she had passed away from an illness.

He knew if he had been able to get the message in time, he might have been able to help prevent his wife's death. So through this heartbreak, he became determined that he would find a way to communicate across distances in a fast method.

That's when Samuel Morse invented the telegraph. Once when he was being interviewed, he was asked if he ever came to a standstill when he was making his experiments and not know what to do.

When he answered yes, his interviewer said, "At such times, what did you do next?" Morse said, "I prayed for more light. And the light came." According to God's promise, He threw more light onto the path so that step by step, Morse could complete the telegraph. That's why the very first message he sent across the telegraph in 1844 were the words, "What God hath wrought" (Numbers 23:23). That means, "What God has created! What God has done!"

God will show you the path to find the answer so you will be saying, "What God has done! It's great. It's wonderful! He has guided me step by step and now I'm right where I want to be."

You can rest assured that every moment of your day is in His hands. Ask Him to throw more light onto your path so you can know the next step to take. Then take it by faith into the answer He has for you.

A Spiritual Powerline to say out loud:
"I TAKE THE NEXT STEP!"

A powerful prayer to pray:
Lord, I believe You direct my way. You hold all my moments in Your hand. Now I ask You to throw some more light onto my pathway. I need to see the next step. And as You unfold my path step by step, I pray to have the faith to take each step. In Jesus' name. Amen.

NOTES:

_____

_____

_____

Day 84

Above Your Highest Dreams

Our dreams are important to us. So, our emotions are wrapped up in them, and sometimes we get a choke hold on them. Yet, the very act of relinquishing those to God is what causes them to happen.

Bob tells how after he was discharged from the Army, he started pursuing his dream of building a great hog farm operation in Indiana. But he didn't have the funds to do it, so in order to provide an income, he took a job in accounting with an industry that was near the farm. Everything was going great. A job, income, and on the side working on the dream of building his hog farm.

That's when God moved on Bob to relinquish his dream to Him and allow Him to fulfill it in His way and timing. That was tough, so

Bob told God that if He wanted him to give up the hog farm at this time, he would have to show him this by not letting any of his eighty sows have babies. It wasn't long until the veterinarian gave Bob the news that every boar he had was sterile. The answer. About that time he read an announcement in a mission magazine that the missions needed an accountant. Bob knew that was his job. He worked for them for 25 years as treasurer.

Just before he retired, a missionary from Honduras approached Bob about helping them start, of all things, a hog operation in that country. Today, Bob and his family live in Honduras and in his words, "We have the hog operation *of my dreams* with four beautiful buildings and a great vocational training program."

When you relinquish to the Lord all you want, from the smallest area of your life to the biggest, He is able to do far over and above your highest dreams (Ephesians 3:20).

A Spiritual Powerline to say out loud:
"MY DREAMS COME TO PASS IN GOD'S HANDS!"

A powerful prayer to pray:
Lord, here are the dreams I have in my heart for my family and health, for my spiritual and financial well-being and my relationships and work—every part of my life small and great. I relinquish all of them to You. I follow Your path in seeing them fulfilled. I know that You will do far over and above what I could ever ask or dream. In Jesus' name. Amen.

NOTES:

_____

_____

_____

Day 85

Even Before You Ask

Even before you ask, God is ready to meet your need. He has made the arrangements and is eagerly waiting to hear your prayer and see your faith.

Dr. Helen Roseveare experienced this in an undeniable way. She was a missionary in an area of Zaire where there were many people with many needs. The facilities were not state-of-the-art to say the least so they had to improvise at times.

She describes how a mother in their mission station had died after giving birth to a premature baby. Although they were in sorrow for her, they quickly had to turn to the challenge of keeping her baby alive. It required an incubator, which they did not have, but they thought perhaps a hot water bottle could do the job. However the only one they had was beyond repair.

So they gathered the children together in the mission station and asked them to pray for the infant and for her sister. As they were praying, one of the girls began to say, "Dear God, please send a hot water bottle today. Tomorrow will be too late because by then the baby will be dead. And dear Lord, send a doll for the baby's older sister so she won't feel so lonely."

Now, how is God going to get a hot water bottle to a mission station in Zaire before the next day and on top of that send a doll so that these little ones can be helped and comforted after the death of their mother? But that child had prayed and God would answer. Even before they asked, He had prepared it.

That very afternoon the mission station received a big package from England. As the missionaries opened it, they saw clothing, which is what they would normally receive, but underneath it all was also a hot water bottle! So when the child who had prayed that prayer saw it, she ran to the big box and began to dig deeper as fast as she could. She was determined to find the doll there for which she had prayed. Sure enough. There was the doll.

Now think about that—to get that package from England, it had to be sent five months prior to the time that mother passed away and the infant would be in need and the sister would need a doll to comfort her. Yet everything was there. That's God. That's how He works. If we allow Him. If we believe.

Imagine the Lord watching over your life and as He does, He sees the need that is coming up; He knows about the experience you will have; He sees the difficulties and challenges that are on their way. Immediately He begins preparing the answer you need, the supply, the encouragement, and the peace. Then He stands up from His throne and begins to listen. For what is He listening? He's waiting to hear your heart's prayer coming to Him filled with faith. He wants to hear that you believe your God will come through.

So in spite of how hard the situation seems, send those words of faith out in prayer. Those words are as light piercing the darkness—the light of hope. God sees that light, and then He responds. You see, He was ready even before you asked. Have strong expectation that the miracle answer is on its way.

A Spiritual Powerline to say out loud:
"MY ANSWER IS ON THE WAY!"

A powerful prayer to pray:
Dear God, You knew what I needed before I did. And I know You have already prepared the answer. So I'm sending forth my faith to You in this prayer. Now, I believe You are releasing that answer into my life. So I praise You for a powerful miracle. In the name of Jesus. Amen.

NOTES:

_____

_____

_____

Day 86

It Will Rise to the Top

Everyone wants what is best for them. When you're making a decision, you try to be sure that you do what is best for you. You don't want to make a choice that would cause you to accept something below what you could have.

But sometimes it can be tough to find the best way. It's not so easy to know which person or product or place is the one for you. If you try to choose before you know that, you can be walking into a very disappointing, troubling condition. So what can you do? How do you find the right one?

I'm sure you've experienced this before where you had to wait until it became evident. That's when God gives you revelation and when He does, what is best is shown! It rises to the top. If you are trying to make a choice or decision on something, as you wait for it to be revealed to you, you start seeing what is best come to the top so it is evident. The cream rises to the top.

God has cream for your life. If you want to partake of it, allow it to rise to the top. That's when you'll see what's best for you. He will reveal it so you know the way to take. You'll know when it's time to "drink"—when it's time to partake of what He has for you. If you start gulping it down too fast before the cream rises, you don't get what is best. You miss out on it. So God is trying to get you to wait until He's formed the cream and revealed to you what is best rises.

Revelation will come so you know the right person or product or place that is for you. Psalm 16:11 promises this: *You will **show me** the path of life; in Your presence is fullness of joy, at Your right hand there are pleasures for evermore.* As God shows you the path to take—what's best for you—that's when you will enter into the fullness of joy. You'll find the pleasures of what He has for your life when you choose what is best.

But you can't choose until He reveals it to you. **You have to wait for what is best to rise to the top and be shown to you.** Don't jump in there and take what is not best. Don't panic and be anxious and allow that to push you into something. Trust God. Trust Him that He has your life in His hands and He will reveal to you *what* you need to know *when* you need to know it. Believe this: God always wants what's best for you. He will not connect you with a person who isn't beneficial for you. He won't have you get a product that isn't right for you. And He won't take you into a place that isn't where you should be. **He wants the best person, product, and place for you.**

The day will come when it will be revealed, and you'll see the work He's been doing.

I was reading a great story about the artist, Michelangelo, that demonstrates how God does this in our lives. He had sculpted an angel out of a piece of marble. It wasn't one of those small cherub types, but it was a strong muscular angel with mighty wings. However when he started, he was just facing a hunk of stone. What God wanted to come from that had to be revealed to him. It had to rise to the top so the vision of that angel could be seen as he began to chip away pieces of marble.

When the masterpiece was finished and he was asked how he did it, Michelangelo responded, "I saw the angel in the marble and carved until I set him free."

That's what God does with your life. He takes a hunk of stone, and He begins to sculpt. He knows what He wants to see in the finished product before He ever begins chipping away what shouldn't be there. He watches as what's best comes to the top. So instead of just one big lump of marble, your life has the best showing in it. You are willing to allow the Master to chip away what shouldn't be a part of your life and bring out what was meant to be there. You allow Him to help you be the best you can be and experience the best. So you have to trust Him when He starts carving and removing something that will not be good for you.

You have to allow His will to rise to the top so you can live as that scripture described: live in the fullness of joy and pleasures because you are where God wants you to be, doing what He wants you to do, and being touched in your life by those He sends to you.

So let the cream rise. Allow what's best for you to come to the top and be revealed by God. He will show it to you because that's what He wants you to experience. The best!

A Spiritual Powerline to say out loud:
"I'M WAITING FOR THE CREAM!"

A powerful prayer to pray:
Lord, I believe my life is in Your hands. You want what is best for me. So I trust You to reveal it to me. I'm letting the cream rise to the top. I receive the best. In the name of Jesus. Amen.

NOTES:

_____

_____

_____

Day 87

Listen for the Sound

What do you do when something has dried up? When finances have evaporated. When the affection in a relationship is almost dead. Energy becomes drained; resources aren't flowing. Something is eating away at peace and joy. The answers to the challenge cannot be found. Something about life does not seem as though it's going to get better.

This is where the Israelites were, but God was about to change everything. He sent the prophet Ezekiel to a place that was filled with dried up bones and told him that those dried bones demonstrated what the people were going around saying: "Our bones are dried up and our hope is lost; we are completely cut off" (Ezekiel 37:11).

They had lost so much that now even their hope was lost. But oh, God was getting ready to revive their hope and show them the future He had planned for them—and He wants to do the same for you.

So, God told Ezekiel to prophesy to the bones. Suddenly there was a thundering noise, shaking and trembling. Bones came together. Then flesh came upon them. He prophesied again and breath and spirit came into them and they stood on their feet as a great host (v. 10). God was showing how He was going to take up the dried bones of their desires and send breath and spirit into them.

No matter how dry something seems, God can revive it. You can go from need to abundance. From disappointment to excitement. From grief and sorrow to joy and peace. What refused to grow will now flourish.

Listen for the thundering—the sound of God's power moving. He is raising up the bones of that situation and giving them breath and spirit. Watch for the miracle breakthrough coming.

A Spiritual Powerline to say out loud:
"I LISTEN FOR THE SOUND OF MY MIRACLE!"

A powerful prayer to pray:
Lord, You see what has dried up in my life. And I believe You are reviving me today. You're moving in my behalf. And You're sending breath and spirit into my situation. I'm listening for the sound of my miracle coming! In the name of Jesus. Amen.

NOTES:

_____

_____

_____

Day 88

The Final Countdown

When a woman is going to have a baby, there is a waiting time before the birth happens. It's the same for *spiritual pregnancy*, which we all experience at different times in our life. When you're pregnant with a desire to be fulfilled or a dream to come to pass or for an answer to be resolved, it's important to understand your condition during that time.

That's what will enable you to successfully have your baby. All those things that are in your heart and spirit that you want to see born can only come about when you are willing to endure the waiting time.

When we compare the natural pregnancy to supernatural pregnancy, we can understand the difficulties that can happen to us during the waiting time. For instance, in the first stages of pregnancy a woman is told she may experience being tired, sick to her stomach, have cravings for certain foods, or the opposite—she may not want certain foods. She will have mood swings, and may have headaches and heartburn and weight gain or weight loss. That's just the first trimester. In the rest of the trimesters, her body will ache and swell, and she will have trouble resting as well as many other things.

Now, think about the stages you experience when you are giving birth to what God has put in your heart. There might be some trouble resting when you're fighting against fear or doubt. There are mood swings. You may have times when your concerns are so great that you eat more and gain weight or the reverse; you can't eat so you lose weight.

But after the doctor has told the mother all the tough things she will experience each trimester, when she gets down to those final weeks, the doctor says, "Now, get excited. The final countdown has begun!" That's what God's Spirit makes known to you in those tough times of pregnancy. When you've been standing in faith and working to keep courage and endure and be strong and have a positive attitude, and you had to fight all the natural symptoms that tried to come, that's when you hear in your spirit, "Now, get excited. The final countdown has begun!" The time is coming when the birth will happen. You're in the final stages.

All the time you're waiting and you're experiencing uncomfortable challenges and emotions, remember why. It's because you have a baby that is going to be born. You're pregnant with what God has put in your heart. It helps the mother to remember when she's experiencing difficult symptoms that the reason why is because she has a baby inside her. It will help you during these difficult times to remember what you have spiritually inside you. Then allow God's Spirit to give you strength and endurance to persevere. God tells us in His Word that the Holy Spirit will help us when we're pregnant with a dream from Him and we're in the waiting stages.

Romans 8 says, *Meanwhile, the moment **we get tired in the waiting,** God's Spirit is right alongside helping us along. If we don't know how or what to pray, it doesn't matter. He does our praying in and for us, making prayer out of our wordless sighs, our aching groans. He knows us far better than we know ourselves, **knows our pregnant condition,** and keeps us present before God. That's why we can be so sure that every detail in our lives of love for God is worked into something good* (Romans 8:26-28 MSG).

The Spirit is with you in every stage of waiting. He's helping you pray and stay in there until the final countdown has begun. It is coming and you want to experience the wonderful moment when your dream is born. Don't miss the birth.

Keep your spirit alert and listening for the time when God says, "Your baby is on the way. Your dream is coming to pass now."

A Spiritual Powerline to say out loud:
"IT'S THE FINAL COUNTDOWN!"

A powerful prayer to pray:
Lord! I am not going to miss the birth of this baby! I believe You give me strength and endurance now to wait. It's the final countdown, and I'm ready to see the fulfillment of the dream You've put in my heart. In the name of Jesus. Amen.

NOTES:

_____

_____

_____

Be Inspired

Your spirit needs to be inspired, especially during the times when you are challenged. Your dream is floundering. Your heart's desire is waning. The responsibilities are getting heavy. The ideas and answers are nowhere to be found. The hardships are pressing down on you. That's why God created inspiration and He created your spirit to require it and respond to it. The Lord wants you to see who you are and what is possible for you to do. Be inspired to believe for your breakthrough.

Day 89

Hi, Special One

There was a man whose spirit was down when he awoke one morning. He was facing so much. You know how it is when you get out of bed and challenges and problems are staring you in the face. You want to crawl back under the sheets and let the day pass. Maybe tomorrow you can face them.

But this man decided to get out of bed. Then he began his prayer time as he always did first in the morning. He began by asking God for help and for a blessing that day. He wanted to know that the Lord cared and was aware of all he was experiencing. Just after the man had prayed this, his son, Timothy, who was almost two years old, came into the room. Timmy had just gotten out of bed and he knew to be quiet in the mornings, because that's when his parents would pray.

Usually he was good at being quiet, but this morning he marched right into his father's room, walked over to him, and put his little hand on top of his dad's folded hands. Then he said, "Hi, special one. Hi, special one." He continued to repeat those words six times. Now, Timothy had never said anything such as that to his father. So the man knew God had sent his son in there with that wonderful message in the midst of his discouragement to tell him that He cared for him and was blessing him.

That's how special you are to God. So when you feel downhearted or overwhelmed as this man was, you can speak out to God and know He will respond. He wants to raise you up so you can go on and see His will accomplished. He doesn't want your head down, but up, watching for the good that's coming.

Sure, you see the bad now, but God already has in motion good things coming to you. Don't just see what is unpleasant or hard; there's more than that—and it's God's hand filled with pleasant blessings and answers for you. He's watching over you as His special one, so of course you're not going to be ignored or forgotten. Just go around the day hearing those words in your mind and heart. God is saying, "Hi, special one!" He wants you to feel His attention on you. Know that you are being heard, and more than that—something is happening because of what you have shared with God. So be expecting to see a great outcome. Watch for what He is doing.

You are His special one. And He doesn't want you to be convinced of anything opposite that. He has too much for you to do and too much He wants to give to your life. That's why **the Lord doesn't want you to spend even one minute of your life entertaining wrong thoughts.** He wants you to hear Him say, "Hi, special one!" Believe that He is right there with you at this very moment, and He is ministering that to your heart.

A Spiritual Powerline to say out loud:
"I'M GOD'S SPECIAL ONE!"

A powerful prayer to pray:
Lord, I believe I am special to You. You're watching over me. Now, I know nothing can overwhelm me. You are sending good into my life. And I'm watching for it! I want to serve You with my life. In the name of Jesus. Amen.

NOTES:

_____

_____

_____

Day 90

You Can Do It and You Will

There are times we may not feel we have the strength to go on in the midst of hard or disappointing conditions. Let's face it; we cannot do much without being strong inside. And if we are downcast or discouraged, it will sap our strength. We won't feel as if we can go on.

There was a student who was telling this to his college advisor. This young man, Mark, had gone to his advisor and just told him upfront, "I can't do this anymore!" Much was against him, the challenges were overwhelming, and he felt he had been beaten.

But his advisor did the best thing he could. He smiled. He wanted this young man to see something positive and so he put a smile on his face and then he said to him, "Mark, you can do this and you will!" There was no room for wondering if he could, or giving him an out. "You can and you will."

That student went on with the reassurance and inspiration he was given that day. His heart was cheered so things weren't so heavy. He knew he could do it, so he graduated and has a good position today. Now in his office is a case that has a memento from his advisor in it. In the case is an actual pair of suspenders that his advisor used to wear before he passed away. Yes, a pair of suspenders. There is much symbolism in that. Because suspenders hold things up. And that's what that advisor was doing for him that day. He was holding him up with encouragement and prayer. That mentor helped to put cheer back in his heart so the heaviness would not keep him down.

The Lord says to you, "You can do this and you will!" He's helping you today to release that heaviness. Push away the sadness and discouragement. Take up the cheer of God and allow it to permeate your mind and heart. As you allow it to infiltrate and push out the heavy bad stuff, then you'll have greater strength. Having cheer makes you stronger. And when you're stronger, what can happen? You can do ANYTHING! You can walk on water!

Isn't that what Peter did? He stepped out of the boat and began to walk toward Jesus who was standing in the midst of the storm out on the water. He could not have done that if he had allowed fear to sap his strength. Fear will hold you back. It will keep you in the boat, screaming, afraid and failing and in need. That's why Jesus said to the disciples when they saw Him, *Be of good cheer; it is I; be not afraid* (Matthew 14:27). **If you have cheer instead of fear in your heart, you're going to step out.** And that's what Peter did.

It wasn't until he allowed fear back into his heart that he started to sink. The scripture says that when he perceived and felt the strong wind—and notice the scripture describes it as "strong"— then he became frightened. He allowed fear to push out the belief that he was stronger than that strong wind. That's when he began to sink and that's when he cried out to the Lord.

Right away Jesus put out His strong arm and caught Peter and raised him up. Then He asked Peter, *Why did you doubt* (Matthew 14:31)? "You were going so well, Peter! You knew I was here. You had pushed fear out of your heart, and you were walking on water. But then you allowed doubt back in so you weren't sure you could do it. You didn't think you could walk on water."

When Jesus told Peter to come out to Him on the water, He was saying, "You can do it and you will do it." The only thing that can steal that kind of message from our hearts is if we allow fear to cause us to doubt the message. **Don't doubt the message.** Don't doubt the word God is giving you.

You will see that need met. You'll watch as things are transformed. Conditions are changed. Challenges are met. Oh, we're talking about a huge turnaround. Great success. You can walk on water!

Second Corinthians 7:6 says that it is God Who encourages and refreshes and cheers the depressed and the SINKING. What does He do for someone who's sinking? He cheers them so they become strong and walk on the storm.

Feel the Spirit of God speaking to you this moment. He's telling you, "You do not have to fear anymore. You are not going to sink. But you're going to walk on the water, because you will be strong in your faith. You *can* do it and you *will* do it."

A Spiritual Powerline to say out loud:
"I CAN DO IT AND I WILL!"

A powerful prayer to pray:
Lord, I'm going to walk on water today. I have Your strength in me so I don't have to stay in the boat and be afraid. I can do anything through You. So I expect mighty miracles and wonderful things to happen. In the name of Jesus. Amen.

NOTES:

_____

_____

_____

Day 91

Heaven on Earth

You know the phrase, "This is heaven on earth"? Have you ever been in a place that was so special that you referred to it as heaven on earth? Maybe when you're with a special person you feel that way. Or perhaps you work with someone who is so good, they make the work place seem like heaven on earth. I won't ask if you work with someone who makes the workplace the opposite.

But you know, we use the phrase, heaven on earth, in a common way. Yet in reality it has great spiritual meaning. As a believer we truly want what is in heaven to happen on earth. We want heaven-on-earth.

When you think about it, what is happening in heaven? Why do we want to have it happen on earth? Because there is blessing, spiritual knowledge, well-being, peace, love, and joy. Everything that's happening in heaven is what God wants for you here on earth.

If you were in heaven right now, you would have no concerns about if God was going to take care of you. You would know every kind of need would be met. That's how He wants you to feel here on earth. That He will take care of you.

Remember Jesus taught us to pray, *Your will be done on earth as it is in heaven* (Matthew 6:10). Just think about all the great things that have been written down in heaven as a plan for your life. When you pray, you're praying those plans down into your existence on earth. **So when events and conditions seem more as if they are hell on earth instead of heaven on earth, start praying heaven into them.**

In Matthew 18, Jesus tells us that whatever we forbid in our life must be what is already forbidden in heaven. In the same sense, whatever we *permit* as God's will for us on earth must be what is already permitted in heaven. In other words, we're praying for heaven on earth.

So you bind what is against God's will for you and you permit what His will in heaven is for you. Don't allow negative thoughts and words to permit what the devil has planned for you to take place. Bind those things that are coming into your life. Disease or lack. Problems in your job or relationships or marriage or family. All the different areas of your life that you're dealing with each day, bind in prayer what is against God's will for you. By your faith, permit heaven's will to be done.

I was reading how a famous man was experiencing a time such as this and how he began to walk out this principle of seeing heaven on earth for his life. You may recognize his name, Darrell Waltrip. Darrell was a professional racing driver. He won the NASCAR cup series several times and so many other racing awards I couldn't name them.

He says that ever since he was twelve years old he got up on the weekends and went to the track, put on a helmet, got behind the wheel of something and raced. He did that for forty-one years. Even when he would think about not racing, a chill would race up and down his spine. He didn't feel he could go on if he wasn't doing this. It was a part of him.

So even when it got to the point that he was past the time that he was winning, he continued to race. He said the last few years of racing were the darkest for him. It felt like hell on earth. That's when he decided to start praying to God, "Your will be done on earth as it is in heaven." And he felt led to start giving fifteen percent of his income to God. Then he started a Bible study in his garage. He stopped whining to God and started asking Him to work His will for him.

When he started doing this, that's when the Lord took care of him. Wonderful things began to happen. He was offered a sports broadcasting position with a network that allowed him to remain in the field of car racing but do something that he enjoyed so much and receive a good salary. Here's how he describes what happened, "I've never imagined that God could have something so much better for me. Broadcasting is the perfect spot at this stage of my life and career. It couldn't be a better fit for a show-off who likes to shoot off his mouth. It keeps me in the sport I love. God had the perfect position waiting for me."

God has something perfect waiting for you also. It will be heaven on earth. He wants to take care of you. Oh hear that in your spirit. God wants to take care of you. Pray for the plans from heaven to come to you on earth where you are right now and where you need them. You can experience the goodness of all the Lord has for you.

A Spiritual Powerline to say out loud:
"I RECEIVE HEAVEN ON EARTH!"

A powerful prayer to pray:
Lord, I know You have wonderful things planned for me in heaven. So I believe now that You will send them into my circumstances. By my faith, I bring heaven on earth into my life. In the name of Jesus. Amen.

NOTES:

_____

_____

_____

Day 92

Don't Use Up Your Resources

God's Word tells us that there must be times that we enter into a time of refreshing. We allow our spirit to be energized and our mind to rest and our body to be invigorated. That will help us overcome discouragement and weariness.

We protect our important resources—our emotions, mind, and body. **Those resources are what we have to help us to perform what God puts in our heart. They enable us to rise above the difficulties and challenges and have the stamina to stay in faith until we receive victory.** So we don't want to keep going until we

227

use up those resources. They are what God has given us and so they are precious cargo. And if we keep going so much we will burn them up. Don't burn your cargo!

There is a story of how a steamboat did this. And it shows how we can do the same. The steamboat started out from shore at Memphis the same time another boat did. The crews of each boat happen to notice one another as they shoved off. So they traveled side-by-side for a while. And then it happened. Some of the sailors from one boat made a comment about how much faster they were than the other one. Of course at that point, they began to egg each other on and challenged their boat against the other boat. That was it. The competition was on!

As they were racing down the Mississippi River, both crews were putting coal in the ovens as fast as they could. They were determined not to be the one behind. But then one of the boats began to drop back. It didn't appear they were going to be able to catch up. That's when one of the men became so desperate that he took some of the cargo on the ship and tossed it into the ovens. When his fellow sailors saw how it burned just as good as coal did, everyone on the boat joined in and began tossing all the cargo in to be burned to create the steam.

And hooray! They won the race. But...they burned their cargo to do it. The very reason for which the boat was in existence was to carry the cargo.

You may be trying hard to win a race, to complete something you desire, to get to the place you want to be. And it frustrates you when you don't seem to be getting there fast enough. It's as though you're falling behind. You want a breakthrough. So what do you do? You work harder. You burn up more energy and mental well-being. Your adrenals get shot. And your emotions aren't there to help you fulfill what you need to do each day. But! You're determined!

Then one day you realize you burned your cargo. Your resources are down. The very thing you desired becomes the problem. You forgot to take time to be refreshed. You took on a burden that became too much because you didn't have anything remaining to help you keep going.

That's why Jesus said that we are to go to Him. Everyone who labors and has burdens must go to Him. When we do, then He says, *I will cause you to rest. [I will ease and relieve and refresh your souls.] Take My yoke upon you and learn of Me...and you will find rest* **(relief and ease and refreshment and recreation and blessed quiet)** *for your souls* (Matthew 11:28, 29).

Can you use some of that right now? Are you burning your cargo in the ovens so that you can have a full head of steam? Think about where you are going to be at the end of it after all your resources are gone.

So what do you think? Is God moving in your heart about some things you can change to help yourself? He can show you the proper boundaries for work and play, for effort and trust, and for activity and rest. Those boundaries help you protect your precious resources. Allow God's Spirit to show you the refreshing that is there for you. That's when you will truly experience all that He has for you.

A Spiritual Powerline to say out loud:
"I AM REFRESHED!"

A powerful prayer to pray:
Lord, show me the way to be refreshed. Help me to fulfill my responsibilities and get through my challenges. Protect my body, mind, and emotions and enable my spirit to be strong. Cause me to be at rest in You. In the name of Jesus. Amen.

NOTES:

_____

_____

_____

Day 93

Getting Back Up

Once a reporter asked Jimmy Ellis, the former Heavyweight World Champion, if he realized of all the world champions who had ever been, Jimmy had been knocked down more times than any of them. You would think that would offend him, but instead he smiled and said, "That just means I got up more times than anyone else." Because he did, he got the prize. The world championship.

In spite of how the circumstances try to knock you back and make you think you cannot go on, you can get back up. God will revive you and help you complete what you need to do because He wants you to receive the final reward. You can experience the tremendous blessing and miracle there for you. You won't be overcome and depleted to the point it's impossible to see done what you desire. You will be revived so you can go on. To revive means to restart. God can re-start you today so you can keep going in spite of the conditions.

This is what God did for the Apostle Paul. He and his coworker, Barnabas, were traveling and preaching the good news of Jesus Christ, and also had done some extensive work in teaching those who were disciples. Eventually, they arrived in a place called Lystra. There they saw a man who could not use his feet. In fact, he had never walked. But as he was hearing what Paul was saying from the Word of God, the Spirit began to give Paul a sense that this man had gained the faith to be healed.

So Paul gazed intently at him and said, *Stand erect on your feet* (Acts 14:10)! The man's faith was ignited with those words. So he got up and began not just to walk around but was jumping. Now, jumping up and down is hard for many people to do period. But think about someone who had never walked from their birth. How unsteady and careful you would think they would be. But there was so much power of God coursing in his body that he had perfect balance. He was made whole that instant. God had rescued him from a life of disappointment.

Now, as all of this was going on, the devil made sure that in the crowd there were some opposing views. He always sends something to try to destroy the good that's happening in our life. So religious leaders, who were against the gospel, persuaded the people to come against Paul. To kill him! So they stoned him and dragged him out of the town, thinking he was dead.

However, disciples who had witnessed what happened formed a circle around Paul. As those disciples prayed, Paul had a miracle recovery. He was revived! He jumped up and went on his way, just as the lame man had done when he prayed for him. It was a restart.

He went on to preach and teach and make disciples of many of the people. Because he had been revived and strengthened, he now established and strengthened the hearts of the believers there. He encouraged them to stand firm in the faith, to keep going in spite of hardships.

That's the encouragement God is sending to you now. Keep going in spite of hardships. He will revive you when the stones have been thrown at you—when the problems have tried to take you out and make you give up.

You can see the work condition turn around, or your living condition. The responsibility will be fulfilled. All of a sudden you will arrive at the end of that trial and see an improvement. You can meet the challenge. Watch as that relationship comes together in a beautiful way. See your spouse act better or your child make good choices.

God knows what you've asked Him for in your heart. When it seems as if it's just not happening and you're too tired to make it happen, be strengthened and encouraged. God is going to send something very special. He is going to send an event or word or gift that will be the trigger to help you be revived. It will restart you. Then you'll go on in full strength, able to see what you desire. That new home or car. That successful business or ministry. Better health. The thing you're facing that needs to be resolved in your favor.

Keep going and believing, because God will see you through. Expect your rescue and then feel the power and strength come into you from the Spirit of God. You are getting a restart so you can get back up!

A Spiritual Powerline to say out loud:
"I'M GETTING BACK UP!"

A powerful prayer to pray:
Father, I have received Your Word, and now I receive Your power. I am revived. Strengthened. Encouraged. I'm ready to get back up and see a miracle happen. This is my restart! In the name of Jesus. Amen.

NOTES:

_____

_____

_____

Day 94

The Road To Fulfilling Your Desire

How many times have you had a longing in your heart, and it was so strong that you felt as if your heart would burst if it was not fulfilled? As time wore on, and you didn't see it come to pass, you may have become sad. It's hard to think about that desire day in and day out and yet see nothing.

God knows we have those desires in our heart. In fact He's the One Who gives them to us so we will pursue them and fulfill His purposes for our lives. But He does not want us to be sad while we are waiting for those to come to pass **because sadness blinds us to the way to take to seeing our desire fulfilled.**

We are to walk that journey to our desire and experience the delight, happiness, and enjoyment He has for us. But notice it is a journey. It's a process. We cannot make the journey and complete it to the fulfillment of our desire if we're downhearted because we haven't seen it yet. That's why Proverbs 13:12 says, *Hope deferred makes the heart sick, but when the desire is fulfilled, it is a tree of life.* We get heartsick when the desire is not fulfilled. But when we have faith, the fulfillment will take over the longing! It will meet the need.

So how do we keep from being sad until the desire comes to pass as God commands us? We trust Him that it will be fulfilled. We travel the road to fulfillment with faith. We get past our emotions and trust. It's only then that we will be able to see the path to take to the completion of our longing. If we are in sadness, we can't see what to do. So we can't make the steps to see God move.

This is what a man discovered when he had a strong desire in his heart to be a writer. He was an attorney but he was sad in his job because he wasn't doing what he felt he was made to do. He didn't know where to begin in order to become an author. He had done many different kinds of jobs, and then gone to college to become an attorney. But he was still dissatisfied. His sadness was keeping him from seeing a way to fulfill his desire. That's what being heartsick can do—it can blind us to the way to receive the very thing we desire.

Then one day he decided he would never start writing unless he took a step. That's when he got on the road to fulfillment. He shook off the sadness and picked up his calendar and in one of the big squares on his calendar, he wrote one word. "Write." W-r-i-t-e. This was a message to himself that he would see each day. So with the word "write" staring at him from his calendar, he decided he was going to go to work sixty minutes earlier each day even though he was already working sixty to seventy hours a week as an attorney. During those first sixty minutes, he was going to write one page per day. That was his first step, and that's what he did.

Each morning, he would be at his desk an hour before his start time, sit there, and write. As he did this, he continued to grow. Where is he today? He's writing novels and has had a New York Times bestseller. He did what we all must do if we want to see any of our desires come to pass. Start the journey and get over our sadness. When we do, we'll be able to see what our first step must be to get where we want to be.

He knew he would never start writing unless he took a step. What is the step you need to take today? Is it hard for you to see because your heart is so sad? You need to get on the journey God has planned for you. Take the step to what you desire and need in your life. You see, even before you can start experiencing it, you need to have joy in spite of what you hate about your life.

There's something you don't like that's going on. And it makes the longing in your heart even stronger. Go into the presence of God and ask Him to fill you with His joy so you can start making positive steps. That's when fulfillment will take over the longing. Yes, actual fulfillment. You can see it happen. Instead of being at the place where you feel you never will see your desire fulfilled, you can live out your dream.

A Spiritual Powerline to say out loud:
"I TAKE THE ROAD TO MY DESIRE!"

A powerful prayer to pray:
Lord, today I refuse to stay in disappointment and sadness. I'm walking down the road to fulfillment. Direct me in each step I am

to take and give me the strength and joy to do it. I see my desire coming to pass. In the name of Jesus. Amen.

NOTES:

_____

_____

_____

Day 95

Are You Tired of It All?

Do you ever feel tired of it all and just want to run? A responsibility or difficulty is getting to be too much. Or maybe you're experiencing a conflict that is wearing on you, or a need or pain. So what do you do?

You keep standing in your faith when you're tired of it all. That's where your strength is. **Continuing to do what you know you must do creates a powerful force to help you through life.** It's when you stop doing the right thing that you begin weakening your position. That's when things start to break down instead of breakthrough. You can go the wrong direction or make the incorrect choice. Then the pain of life just becomes greater.

That's what the man David experienced in the Bible (I Samuel 21). He had been anointed by the prophet, Samuel, to be the next King of Israel. But the present King of Israel, Saul, decided he was going to change that. So he began to pursue David to try to put him out of the way. Running from Saul began to wear on David. It got real old.

You know how something can get old after a while. We become tired of the spiritual warfare. Praying. Believing. Standing in faith. When we start feeling that way, that's when fear can try to take over. It convinces us that this will never turn around. We will go on forever having this issue, dealing with that problem, being overwhelmed by this these duties or that disappointment or those conditions. We're tempted to doubt if God will take care of what concerns us and complete it. It doesn't feel as though we will ever win this.

Because David was feeling that way, he decided to run and when he did, he went straight to the city of Gath. Now, to show you how desperate he was to get away from it all, the city he went to was the hometown of the Philistine giant, Goliath, whom he had killed in conflict. So when David arrived there, Achish, who was the Philistine ruler over the city, was told by his servants that they recognized this was David, their enemy.

That's when David came up with the idea to change his behavior before them and pretend to be insane. The reason he did this is because in those ancient times, those who were considered insane were protected. So David felt that if he changed his behavior, he would be protected from the Philistines taking him as prisoner and perhaps killing him. He began to scribble on the doors of the gates and drool into his beard.

Can you believe he has been reduced to this? That's to where fear and fatigue will take us. Instead of standing in the strength of our faith and being powerful before the enemy, we are reduced to coming up with our own means for getting out of situations. We become weak and desperate.

When Achish saw this once strong, powerful, and celebrated man acting insane, he told his servants that he was mad and they should not have brought David to him. He didn't want him in his house. So David was allowed to depart, and he escaped to a cave. It was there that those who knew him and of his anointing began to gather to him and he became strong once again.

When God sees fear and fatigue taking over, He helps us to become strong again. We're able to stand and see what He will do to help and sustain us until our answer comes, and we see victory. Because David chose to stand before Saul and wait until God put him on the throne, he eventually became the King of Israel—the best king Israel ever had.

So much is waiting for you. It's good. It's what the Lord desires for your life. So when you're tired of it all—all the hassle or disappointments, all the conflict or pain or need—that's when you need to ask Him to help you to continue to stand. Allow Him to help you overcome fear and fatigue so you can experience what is waiting for you.

You can do this—you can stand in your place until you see the breakthrough. Believe you'll experience the fulfillment of what God has put in your heart.

A Spiritual Powerline to say out loud:
"I'M STRONG IN FAITH!"

A powerful prayer to pray:
Lord, I ask You to strengthen me to stand. I am not tired and weak, but I am strong in You. Fear and fatigue are pushed out of my life. I overcome this and now I will see the good things You have waiting for me. In the name of Jesus. Amen.

NOTES:

_____

_____

_____

Day 96

See It to the Finish

It's been said that there are two kinds of people in the world. The can-dos and the will-dos.

The can-dos are those who have the ability to do something but they won't stick with it and finish. The will-dos get the job done! They refuse to be denied what they're after. They will finish the job so they can accomplish their aim.

Now, because of the Spirit of God within you, you are a will-do person. You won't quit until your faith has pulled you through. You will finish what you're after. You're just as a cross-country runner— they go the distance until they finish the race.

I don't know if you know much about cross-country running but in my opinion it's a grueling sport. Instead of running on a track, the person runs on land. That means they have to cross over all kinds of terrain. And it seems they run forever. It's not a sprint, in other words.

There was a man who was telling how he tried out for the cross-country team when he was in high school. What amazed him was that after the run was over, the guys who were already on the team were just fine when they finished the race. But when he tried it, he felt he was dying and couldn't finish. He gave up with a mile yet to go. So he asked the coach about it, and his response was that the great runners understand that their will gives out before their bodies. So they use their will to persevere and finish even though their bodies are saying to quit. **Then this man understood the race wasn't just about strength, but it was about your will.**

You must determine within yourself you will not be stopped. That may be where you are concerning something you need to see happen. You're ready to come to the place within yourself that you won't be denied what you've been waiting for—you are a will-do person.

But it may feel as though you're running cross country. You feel the sweat and it's been a long time that you've been working at it, and maybe some things are starting to hurt. Just as a runner starts to hurt in their muscles, you may be experiencing that in your heart. You're tired and you still don't see the finish. So God is going to help you today to get to the finish. Let your heart be encouraged and feel the spiritual energy the Lord is sending to you. You can see this to victory! As you seek the Lord, determine you will not be denied what you are after.

Have you ever heard of that old song, "I Would Not Be Denied"? One verse says, "As Jacob in the days of old, I wrestled with the Lord; and instant with a courage bold, I stood upon His Word. I would not be denied, I would not be denied, till Jesus came and made me whole, I would not be denied." (Ref. Genesis 32:26.)

That song was written by Charles Jones and it came to him after he had spent a night wrestling in prayer. He was going through some tough trials and tests. He said, "I prayed in every closet, behind every door; wherever I could hide I went to my knees begging for mercy. But no comfort came. Satan tempted me to despair. [But finally] my mourning became a song. When all the trial was over, thinking of it all one day while alone communing with God and thanking Him for His mercy to me, my soul felt that it must express itself in song; and so was born 'I Would Not Be Denied.'"

Jones had the tremendous victorious feeling of how it is after you wrestle in prayer and receive a breakthrough. When he got his breakthrough, that song was born. He refused to be denied and therefore he would not despair, but his grieving was turned to singing. He saw God do a work in his behalf. He prayed until he got the job done.

That's what you can do right now. Wrestle in prayer until you get a breakthrough for your desire. Be a will-do person. That's when you will begin to see victory. The work will be done. You will see it to the finish!

A Spiritual Powerline to say out loud:
"I'M SEEING IT TO THE FINISH!"

A powerful prayer to pray:
Lord, I am going to see this to the finish. I will not miss what You have for me. My heart is encouraged as I shout, "I will not be denied!" Victory is mine! In the name of Jesus. Amen.

NOTES:

_____

_____

_____

Day 97

Don't Put Up With the Opposition

Wouldn't life be wonderful if we had no opposition? Nothing to oppose our healing, our prosperity, our growth in God. We never had a problem in our relationships or with accomplishing our work.

But we know that if we are breathing, our enemy, the devil, is going to make sure that we experience resistance to what we want to do in our life. Everything good God sends to us is going to meet with an opponent. It will be conditions or problems or disappointments. They can wear you down and you can come to the place you are about ready to give up something that should be yours. Unless! You decide you won't put up with opposition. You stand in the face of what is taking something that is yours. You keep doing what God has put in your heart even as you are dealing with what is opposing you.

You won't give into the circumstances or people that try to take away what you want to see in your life. You get right in the face of the opposition. Show them you're going to keep standing and protect what is yours.

I want to give you the most vivid picture of how it looks to do this. You may have seen or heard of the TV series called, *The Andy Griffith Show*. It ran for about eight years in the 60s and was a nostalgic type program. On the Internet, there is an episode where the young son of Andy has to face a bully who keeps taking his milk money from him.

The son's name is Opie, and every day Aunt Bee makes Opie his peanut butter and jelly sandwich for lunch and gives him a nickel to buy milk at school. But a bully meets him on the way to school each day and takes his nickel, so he has to eat the peanut butter and jelly sandwich dry, without milk. Life is tough for Opie.

Then one day his father discovers what has been happening even though Opie has never told him. So he decides to tell his son a story of how when he was a boy and he had to face a bully once when another boy was trying to take away his favorite fishing hole. Because he stood up to him and refused to give up what was his, today he is still enjoying his favorite place to fish.

So Opie took in all of this and decided he was going to stand up to the bully who had been stealing his money. The day came and even though the other boy tried to intimidate and hurt Opie, he stood in the face of his opposition. So the bully backed down and Opie got to spend his nickel for milk that day. Then he rushed to his dad's office and told him all about it. He ended with these good words, "You want to know something, Pa, a sandwich sure tastes better with milk."

Are you choking down a sandwich without your milk? Don't give your nickel over to the bully. Stand in the face of opposition and believe you can have what is yours.

Don't give up your milk money, your favorite fishing hole, your health or finances or family. Keep standing until you get that promotion or the problem solved, or that "something new" that you need in your life. The bully, the devil, wants you to choke on what he is trying to cram down your throat and make you accept it. Refuse to accept it.

God is with you and will help you get what will make your life better—all those things that have been determined for you by His giving and merciful hand. You're going on to achieve what's in your heart. See dreams come to pass. God wants you to walk into a land flowing with milk and honey (Deuteronomy 27:3).

The opposition will try to take from you what God has planned to give to you, but when the resistance comes, the Lord will help you stand in the face of it so you have victory. **You will outlast the opposition and that's when your sandwich will taste so good, because...it's better with milk!**

James 4:7 tells us to do this, *Yell a loud "no" to the devil and watch him scamper. Say a quiet "yes" to God and He'll be there in no time* (MSG).

Be at peace. Don't allow the opposition to cause you to sit down, but keep standing because your victory day is coming. **The opposition is *going down.* And you are going up.** You will have the works of God operating in your behalf.

A Spiritual Powerline to say out loud:
"I WILL NOT PUT UP WITH THIS!"

A powerful prayer to pray:
Father, I am standing against the opposition today. I know You are here for me. The opposition is going down, and I am going up. I will experience the triumph You have for me. In the name of Jesus. Amen.

NOTES:

_____

_____

_____

Day 98
_____

Your Work Will Be Rewarded

We know that life is not all fun and entertainment. There has to be some hard work going on at times. If we want something to be successful and fulfilling, then we have to make some sacrifice.

That's how it is with everything worthwhile. Hard work and sacrifice are required. However, God wants you to know this: on the other side of your hard work and sacrifice are great reward and blessing and fulfillment.

So when you feel that what you're doing is getting harder, have faith for this: God is going to take you to the time when you'll experience the reward of what you are doing. Whenever you do the work the Lord has for you in any area, there is recompense and the beautiful and great final product of your work.

The man, Asa, in the Bible is a good example of this. Asa had just taken over reigning over Judah at a time when some hard work had to be done in order to help Israel follow the true God. So he took away the foreign altars and the high places. He also broke down the statues to the goddess and commanded Judah to seek God and obey His commandments. He repaired the altars and the worship places. Then to protect the territory from enemies, he built fortified cities with walls, towers, gates, and bars. In other words, he was working hard.

So God sent a prophet to him by the name of Azariah and he described to the King how the Lord had been with him the whole time he was doing all of these good things. Then this is how the prophet ended his discourse. *Be strong, therefore, and let not your hands be weak and slack, for your **work shall be rewarded*** (II Chronicles 15:7).

When Asa heard those words, he took courage and God rewarded all he did. He had favor and the people gathered to him because they saw the Lord was with him. Then they all entered into the covenant with God, and the Bible says they were given rest and peace from their enemies.

Your work shall be rewarded! Hear that today. When you feel tired and weak, the Lord can give you energy and help you stay strong. Keep working hard, so you will be rewarded.

Second Timothy 2:6 says that it's the hard-working farmer who gets to partake of the first share of the fruits. They're not the last one to receive. They're the first one.

The effort you are putting in on that relationship or that job can produce. The efforts you make toward getting out of debt or increasing your financial well-being may require sacrifice, but you will enjoy the rewards of that. You can partake of the harvest of emotional balance, and coming out of that depression or discouragement. When you work hard to solve an issue, it will create a time of rejoicing. The work for better health can produce feeling well, receiving good medical reports, and being able to do more.

God will give you the grace and strength you need to work as hard as necessary in order to fulfill His purpose. The Apostle Paul said he worked harder than all the other apostles, but he also said, *It was not really I, but the grace of God that was within me* (I Corinthians 15:10).

You are putting forth the effort by God's power. So you can experience what He has prepared for you. Hard work and sacrifice help develop character and dependability and responsibility. It shapes your faith and dependence on God instead of someone else. It's just a good feeling!

So the Lord sends encouragement to you today that all the hard work you're doing right now and the sacrifices you're making are producing some great results that you will experience soon.

Whatever He has given you to accomplish, look forward to the reward. It's going to be fulfilling when you see the product your work and sacrifice have produced. You can experience how good you feel after you reduce your weight, the growth you recognize inside yourself when you handle conflict with maturity, the reward of seeing a plan come together, a family come together, a body of believers joining to accomplish good things. He's there to help you with that child, that challenge, that business and ministry.

Good things take good work. Remember that, when your body and emotions are tired. Allow God to give you strength to go on and have a good attitude as you work. Yes, you're going to make it to the other side to see what God has waiting for you.

A Spiritual Powerline to say out loud:
"MY WORK WILL BE REWARDED!"

A powerful prayer to pray:
Thank You, God, for the grace and strength You give me to work hard. Now I expect great results and fulfillment from what I am doing. Good things are coming from my good work. I believe this. In the name of Jesus. Amen.

NOTES:

_____

_____

_____

Day 99

Keep the Pace With God

Have you ever gone walking or jogging with someone and you couldn't keep up? They set the pace and it was just a bit too fast for you. Or they went so far that you became too tired to keep up. So you figured out that if you were going match their pace you had to get in better shape or get left behind.

I got tickled when I was reading about how this happened for a man named Dave who was training to do a 5K run. He didn't want to train by himself, so he took his wife out on a trail that they had enjoyed taking in the past. Each time they would start out just walking. Then he would get her to pick up the pace with him to go faster.

One day when they were doing this, after about half a mile into the trail, they saw a young woman coming from the other direction. Her ponytail was whipping back and forth. Earbuds in. Perfect exercise outfit on. As she sprinted toward them, she was coming so fast, they had to jump out of the way as she blew right past them.

Well, Dave decided he could not allow that. He felt that he had to compete. So he turned to his wife and said, "It's time to pick up the pace." Soon they started going faster down the path. After they had gone about half an hour, here came the same young woman. He couldn't believe it. That meant she had been around the trail already once and was now lapping them.

He said to his wife, "It's *on* now!" He picked up the pace and was almost dragging his wife behind him. So by the time they arrived at the end of the trail, he was feeling pretty good. He had gone fast enough that the young woman would never catch up. But all of a sudden, she appeared and blew past them again. That made him downright mad. He began to scream, "This is ridiculous." Then it dawned on him that if he was going to keep the same pace as that young woman, he was going to have to make a greater commitment to training.

God has set a pace for your life. If you are going to keep up with it, you have to have the commitment level. It takes spiritual commitment to make it. That means you stay full of the Spirit of God. Indulge in His presence and His Word so that it builds you up.

If you don't keep up the pace with God, He can't do all the things He wants to do *with you and for you.*

So if you don't want to get left behind, and if you want to realize the desires of your heart that He's placed there and see things accomplished, and walk into the miracle answers He has for you—KEEP THE PACE. Make sure you have within you what you need from His Spirit to keep strong and have endurance and perseverance. That's what happens when you stay full of the Spirit of God. You can endure until you finish and see God's purpose fulfilled.

It's when you try to set the pace for yourself that you can miss out on His timing. You're not able to see what He has for you to do and receive. He must be allowed to determine the speed that things are going to go.

Romans 3: 27, 28 tells us how this works. It says, *What we've learned is this: God does not respond to what <u>we</u> do; we respond to what <u>God</u> does. We've finally figured it out. Our lives get in step with God and all others by letting Him set the pace, not by proudly or anxiously trying to run the parade* (MSG). That's our job—to get in step with God; not to ask Him to get in step with us. We don't get into pride and try to run the parade of our life.

Neither do we get into fear and become anxious and try to determine the speed things will go. When we don't have what we need yet, we may begin to feel He's not keeping pace with us! But the point is He is not supposed to keep pace with us.

We have to get in step with Him if we want to see His will fulfilled. In order to do that, we have to be full of His Spirit. Hear His voice and recognize the leading of the Spirit. It's as we stay full that we are able to persevere and endure to the end.

Oh, there's so much that God does not want you to miss. He has so many good things to do for you and with you. Keep the pace. Make the commitment to stay full so you can go fast enough. You'll be able to persevere and endure until you see the fulfillment of what He has ahead for you.

A Spiritual Powerline to say out loud:
"I'M KEEPING PACE WITH GOD!"

A powerful prayer to pray:
Lord, I'm ready to keep the pace with You. I make that commitment today. I want You to fulfill everything You want to do for me and with me. So, I believe I will see growth and goodness and miracle answers come to my life. In the name of Jesus. Amen.

NOTES:

_____

_____

_____

Day 100

God Is Sending Something New

In God's Word, He says, *See! I make all things new!* (Ref. Revelation 21:5.) That's what He wants to do for your life now. He can take you out of what isn't working and show you the power of what can be done.

Don't be hesitant to believe for God to take you into something new. You know, we can get into a rut of believing that the answer we need has to come in a certain way. We get focused on it. **God has to come along and show us a new way and see if we're willing to have faith for it.**

This is what He did with a man who was ill. John chapter 5 describes how this man had been watching for his breakthrough from a disorder for thirty-eight years.

Since he was not mobile, he stayed by a pool called Bethesda with other people who were suffering. Some manuscripts say that the people were there because they believed an angel would come down unannounced and stir the water in the pool. Then whoever was the first one to get into it would be the one to receive their healing. This man had become focused on this way as his only answer.

So Jesus went up to this hurting disappointed person and asked him, *Do you want to become well? Are you really in earnest about getting well?* (Ref. John 5:6.) He was asking him this so He could remove his attention off the old way to get his need met and get him to see the new way to his answer. Obviously, from day to day he experienced disappointment and discouragement from not being able to get his healing. His hope was waning, so Jesus had to stimulate his hope.

And sometimes God will come to you with a word—oh you know how it is—you've received those words before from Him that stimulated your hope. In fact, you didn't even realize how dead you were on the inside to believe something new could happen for you. But when God gave you a word, and He touched your heart and spoke to your spirit, it sparked something. It stimulated new hope that *maybe just maybe God is speaking to me about this, and He is ready to do something.*

That's what He's doing right now. **He's giving you a word to get you prepared for the "new" that is coming.**

Now, this is when YOU have to do something. Step out in faith and believe for a new beginning. This thing, this old problem or issue is going to be gone and there will be a breakthrough just as Jesus was about to do for this man who was sitting hopeless and helpless with his need.

In essence He said to the man, "Here's your answer right now. Do something new. Get up! Pick up your bed and walk!" This man could have rejected that. He could have been so down and filled with doubt that he would not do it.

But when God says, "It's time. Get up. Do something new. Have faith to do what I'm telling you to do," that's when we must take the opportunity. Our fresh start is here ready for us to enter into it.

The Bible says instantly, I mean he didn't waste any time, but instantly that man picked up his bed and recovered his strength and took off walking. I imagine he did not stop walking for quite a while. It felt fresh and new to him. He felt more alive. He could do what he could not do before. Go and see things he had not seen for thirty-eight years because he could not walk. His opportunity had come and the wait was over.

Have you tried but you have not been able to find the answer to the breakthrough you need? Things may have been this way for a long time. You just don't have the means to make it happen, you don't feel strong enough to make it happen. You can't find the right resources or opportunity. God is coming to you with new opportunity. The opportunity to believe for your miracle. Do something new. Get up. Have faith that you are receiving your answer.

Pick up your bed and walk—walk right into the fresh start He has for you. Oh hallelujah, think of that. The conditions are changing in your favor because Jesus has walked up to you as He did to that man to show you the power He has to change conditions.

Get ready for conditions to change in your life. Get ready for God to say, "SEE! I MAKE ALL THINGS NEW." Your hope is being stimulated to believe for "something new" to take place. It will knock away what has been the problem and the issue, and the something new will replace it. That's what God has for you. Believe for it.

A Spiritual Powerline to say out loud:
"SOMETHING NEW IS COMING!"

A powerful prayer to pray:
O Lord, today new hope is stimulated in me. I believe Your word that something new is coming. I will receive my answer. I have faith for that. In the name of Jesus. Amen.

NOTES:

_____

_____

_____

Get a Word of Power for Your Life!

John and I are here to feed you God's Word, grow your faith, and pray for you in a powerful and personal way. Get the help God wants to give you as you face storms and challenges and just everyday responsibilities and hassles. Listen to Word of Power *teachings and share with us how you want us to pray with you in a personal way. After we pray we'll send you some words of hope and encouragement that will come from God's Spirit for your life!*

Jeanne and John Alcott

Three ways you can listen to *Word of Power* teachings with JEANNE ALCOTT:
- ✓ Listen on radio or download them at www.AlcottMinistries.org. For a radio broadcast schedule go to our Web site or write.
- ✓ Have four CDs delivered to you each month (available on Web site or call).
- ✓ Listen on iTunes.

Jeanne Alcott
Alcott Ministries
PO Box 3400
Broken Arrow, OK 74013
918-459-9191
www.AlcottMinistries.org

This Is Your Day!

You're very special and dear to God and that is why He's coming to you at this moment. If you don't know His Son, Jesus Christ, as your Savior this is your day. You can receive eternal life and walk in the good plans He has for you. Be bold and daring and take that step at this moment and see how it transforms your life and gives you peace and joy you've never known.

God is reaching out to you in His kindness and goodness to invite you to open up your heart to Him. Receive forgiveness and feel the freedom that comes into your life.

At this moment, just pray these words to God from your heart:
"Dear God, I believe Jesus Christ is Your Son. I receive Him into my heart now as my Savior. Forgive my sins and give me a new life. I believe I will walk in the good plans You have for me every day, and someday I will have eternal life in heaven with You. I belong to You. In the name of Jesus. Amen."

Oh My Friend, you have so much to look forward to now! It's just the beginning of all the good God is going to do for you. Live in the blessing and purpose He has for you—every day of your life and for eternity in heaven. God cares for you so much and wants to show you the good things waiting for you. So we encourage you to attend a Bible-based church and read God's Word and pray. And as you tell us that you have prayed that prayer, we will send you some materials to read that will encourage and empower you. So let us know today. We want to rejoice with you and stand with you in prayer!

Jeanne and John Alcott

Sources for 100 Days to Your Breakthrough

Day 1
The story about the cab driver and the statue is from www. sermoncentral.com. Accessed 12/17. Source: "Part One—Tenth Hours" by Russell Brownworth, January 19, 2009.

Day 4
The story of the boy climbing the tree is from www.preachingtoday. com. Accessed 9/13. "Child Learns To Focus Upwards."

Day 5
The information about Chuck Yeager breaking the sound barrier is from www.chuckyeager.com. Accessed 3/17. And from www. sermoncentral.com. Accessed 3/17.

Day 6
The story about Richard Evans is from www.richardpaulevans.com. Accessed 7/16. "The boy who dared to be great."

Day 8
Adapted from www.preachingtoday.com. Accessed 12/12. "We Were Born to Give" David B. Jackson, "Leadership."

Day 10
The story about Knute Rockne's team is from www.preachingtoday. com. Accessed 4/13. "Coach Intimidates Opponents With Trickery" Steve May, sermonnotes.com.

Day 11
The story about Colonel Harland Sanders is from www.wikipedia. org. Accessed 11/17. And www.snopes.com. Accessed 11/17.

Day 12

The story about Jeff and Julie and the carpentry business is from www.preachingtoday.com. Accessed 2013. "Debt-ridden Couple Learns to Give First to God" from sermon "Here Is My Investment Strategy" by Davey Ferguson, pastor of Community Christian Church in Naperville, Illinois, 11/26/01.

Day 13

The story about the woman being healed in her knee is from www. cbn.com. Accessed 5/17. "Need Pain Unable To Stop Dance Ministry."

Day 16

The story about Winston Churchill is from www.sermoncentral.com. Accessed 11/17. Two articles. And from www.visitpearlharbor.org. Accessed 1/18.

Day 19

The story about the trainer and the tigers is from *The Treasury of Bible Illustrations* by Ted Kyle and John Todd/page 160.

Day 21

The story about the puppies in the chickens is from www. sermoncentral.com. Accessed 4/16. "Do You Fear What You Need Not Fear?" from the sermon, "Running With a Limp" by Ty Tamasaka, September 9, 2011.

Day 23

The story about Jodi was taken from www.preachingtoday.com. Accessed 07/12. "Girl Shows Courage in Haiti" by Mike Breaux, pastor of Heartland Community Church, Rockford, Illinois, in a sermon at Willow Creek Community Church 5/26/02.

Day 25

The story about the Prince and the wounded man is from *A Treasury of Bible Illustrations* by Ted Kyle and John Todd/page 34.

Day 27

The story about Chesapeake Bay and picaroons is from www. nytimes.com. Accessed 7/15. "Father and Son Fishing Trip on the Chesapeake Bay" by Tim Neville.

Day 28
The story about Bill being healed is from www.sermoncentral.com. Accessed 5/16. By David Phaneuf. The minister's name is Norm but no last name was given.

Day 29
The story about Jack and the bully is from www.sermoncentral.com. Accessed 5/15. By Scott Weber. Adapted from "Fuzzy Memories" by Jack Handey.

Day 31
Information about Marine training for ambushes is from www.sermoncentral.com. Accessed 11/16. By Chris Surber.

Day 32
The story about Oscar Eliason is from www.wikipedia.org. Accessed 7/15. And from www.sermoncentral.com. Accessed 6/15. By Johnny Creasong. Note: the story in Sermon Central seems to have some errors in it, whereas Wikipedia quotes from a piece written by Oscar Eliason himself. I did not use the erroneous parts from Sermon Central.

Day 33
The story about David Livingstone is from www.sermoncentral.com. Accessed 5/15. "The Mission of David Livingstone" from the sermon, "Putting Your Heart Where Your Money Is" by Bob Joyce, 8/4/11.

Day 34
The story about the American troops in the Gulf War is from *1001 Illustrations That Connect* by Craig Brian Larson and Phyllis Ten Elshof/page 317. Also used in WOP #1275.

Day 35
The story and information about the 1924 Mount Everest expedition is from www.sermoncentral.com. Accessed 2/16. By Mark Brunner. Source is from "Doing Your Part" by Gene Getz, Regal, 1984, pages 152, 153. And from www.wikipedia.org. Accessed 2/16.

Day 36
The story about the Tsunami in India is from www.preachingtoday. com. Accessed 11/13. "Old Seawall Saves City From Tsunami" source is from an article by Chris Tomlinson, Associated Press 1/05.

Day 38
The quote by Corrie ten Boom is from www.preachinglibrary.net. Accessed 12/15.

Day 39
The story about Washington crossing the Delaware is from www. sermoncentral.com. Accessed 1/16. By J. Martin. And from www. sermoncentral.com. Accessed 3/16. "Prayer and Cadwalader" by Perry Greene.

Day 41
Most of the story about Conrad Hilton is from the video that is shown in the Hilton Hotels that I watched. I believe it was in 2009. The quote by Conrad Hilton concerning Eddie Fowler is from *Be My Guest* by Conrad Hilton/page 261.

Day 42
The story about Michelle and the car accident is from www. sermoncentral.com. Accessed 2/18.

Day 43
The quote about problems and dreams is from *The Speaker's Quote Book* by Roy B. Zuck/page 553. Also used in WOP #1573.
The story about Frank and the fish is from www.sermoncentral.com. Accessed 1/18.

Day 45
The quote by the baseball manager is from www.sermoncentral. com. Accessed 10/18. It is quoting Leo Durocher.

Day 47
The information about cartographers and the ancient maps is from www.sermoncentral.com. Accessed 11/17. "Afraid of the Unknown." Source: sermon, "Mary—A Song of Trust" by Ed Rowell, www. preachingtoday.com.

Day 48
The story about the woman having brain surgery is from *A Treasury of Bible Illustrations* by Ted Kyle and John Todd/pages 368, 369.

Day 49
The story about Louis Mayer is from www.sermoncentral.com. Accessed 1/16. By Anne Grant. From "The Echo," The Guideposts Anthology, ed. Norman Vincent Peale, Pawling, New York: Guideposts Associates, 1953, pages 209-to 12.

Day 51
The story about Thomas Chisholm is from www.sermoncentral. com. Accessed 10/16. By R. David Reynolds. Source: *Amazing Grace: 366 Inspiring Hymn Stories for Daily Devotions* by Kenneth W. Osbeck, Grand Rapids, Kregel Publications, 1990, page 348.

Day 52
The story about Steve and the penny is from www.preachingtoday. com. Accessed 7/15. "The Value of a Penny" from the files of *Leadership*, by Steve Sjogren.

Day 53
The story about the two girls jumping off the table is from www. sermoncentral.com. Accessed 4/16. "God Will Catch You" by Dale Pilgrim.

Day 54
The story about Ernie Harwell is from www.preachingtoday.com. Accessed 1/14. "Sports Announcer Ernie Harwell Loves Christ More Than Baseball" by Greg Asimakoupoulos from a telephone interview with Ernie Harwell and articles by Pat Zacharias of the *Detroit News.*

Day 56
The story about the boy singing to his baby sister is from www. sermoncentral.com. Accessed 2/16. "The Brother's Song" by Bill Butsko.

Day 57
The story about Todd Skinner and Trango Tower is from www. preachingtoday.com. Accessed 8/15. "Rock Climbers Learn to 'Get on the Wall'" adapted from *Great Work* by David Stuart, McGraw-Hill, 2014, pages 160-163.

Day 58
The information about young athletes having more injuries is from www.preachingtoday.com. Accessed 2/15. "Lack of Rest Causes a Spike in Athlete Injuries" from "Anterior cruciate ligament tears plague teenage athletes…" *The New York Post*, 8/20/13 and from "Of ACLs, Tommmy Johns, and 'One Fine Day,'" by Howie Espenshield, Mbird blog.

Day 59
The story about Jimmy and Davey in the rip current is from www.preachingtoday.com. Accessed 11/12. "John Ortberg on Following God Instead of Your Gut" from the sermon, "The Way of Wisdom."

Day 60
The story about the man getting leeches is from www.preachingtoday.com. Accessed 6/15. "Bathing in God's Forgiveness" from "Character Forged From Conflict" by Gary Preston, Bethany, 1999.

Day 62
The story about a small town in Austria and Napoleon's army is from www.sermoncentral.com. Accessed 11/15.

Day 63
The story about the woman with surgery on her mouth is from www.sermoncentral.com. Accessed 11/15. By Robert Leroe from "Mortal Lessons." No information is given as to what publication "Mortal Lessons" is. The doctor was Richard Selzer, MD.

Day 64
The story about the research study concerning food and office binder clips is from www.newyorker.com. Accessed 7/15. "The Good, the Bad, and the Hungry" by Nicola Twilley 3/15.

Day 65
The story about the man purchasing the van is from www.sermoncentral.com. Accessed 9/18.

Day 66
The story about making maple syrup is from www.sermoncentral.com. Accessed 10/16. "Refining Sap to Maple Syrup" by Michele Straubel, Red Lake, Minnesota, from the sermon "Our Living Hope, by C. Philip Green, April 26, 2011. Also used in WOP #2058.

Day 67

The information about this and Francis Schaeffer is from www. wikipedia.org. Accessed 1/15. And *Courageous Christians* by Joyce Vollmer Brown/pages 111, 112.

Day 68

The story about the father and son cutting down the tree is from www.sermoncentral.com. Accessed 7/17. Source: "Tough Times Never Last, but Tough People Do!" By Robert H. Schuller, Thomas Nelson.

Day 72

The story about the national baseball player and the manager and stealing base is from www.sermoncentral.com. Accessed 2/18. Source: *How Life Imitates the World Series* by Thomas Boswell. The player was Reggie Jackson and the manager was Earl Weaver of the Baltimore Orioles.

Day 74

The story about the woman praying for the guests of the church is from www.sermoncentral.com. Accessed 10/17. "Hidden Prayer Results in Revival.") Source: *Don't Underestimate Your Prayers* sermon by Philip Harrelson, August 6, 2010.

Day 75

The story about the widow and three kids is from www.sermoncentral. com. Accessed 8/17.

Day 76

The story about Leonard Dober and David Nitschmann is from www. ctlibrary.com. Accessed 3/15. And from the original source for which I do not have the name, but it is probably in one of my older books.

Day 77

The story about the woman being married in her thirties is from www. boundless.org. Accessed 6/17. "Why You Should Keep Hoping for Marriage" by Suzanne Hadley Gosselin, April 27, 2015.

Day 78

The story about the grapes is from www.sermoncentral.com. Accessed 3/16. "When God Makes You Wait" submitted by David

Finch. From *It Happens After Prayer* by H. B. Charles, Moody Publishers, 2013, page 37.

Day 80
The story about the church being moved by the flood is from www.preachingtoday.com. Accessed April/15. "Church Finds Miraculous New Home" by Dale Fredin, as reported to and written by Barb Lee in *The Highland Church Highlighter*, January-December issue, 2014.

Day 81
The story about the monk is from www.preachinglibrary.com. "The Sleeping Monk" June 2013.

Day 82
The story about Sean and Nikki is from www.cbn.com. Accessed 12/15.

Day 83
The poem about God leading is from *The Speaker's Quote Book* by Roy B. Zuck/page 239/Barbara C. Ryberg. Also used in WOP #1737. The story about Samuel Morse is from www.illustrations.com. Accessed 11/15. And from www.wikipedia.org. Accessed 11/15.

Day 84
The story about Bob and the hog farm is from www.preachingtoday.com. Accessed 1/15. "In Hog Farm Heaven" from "Called to Prayer" by Bob Hudson; reprinted in *Men of Integrity* 10/25/01.

Day 85
The story about the children, the missionary, a hot water bottle, and doll is from www.sermonillusrations.com. Accessed 8/15.

Day 86
The story about Michelangelo and the angel statue is from www.sermoncentral.com. Accessed 5/18.

Day 89
The story of Timothy and his dad is from *1001 Illustrations That Connect* by Craig Brian Larson and Phyllis Ten Elshof/page 315.

Day 90

The story about the mentor and the student is from www. sermoncentral.com. Accessed 7/18. By Mark Schaeufele. The mentor was Dr. Gary McGee.

Day 91

The story about Darrell Waltrip is from *Darrell Waltrip One-on-One* by Darrell Waltrip and Jay Carty/Day 50, Gospel Light, Ventura, California, 2004. And from www.wikipedia.org. Accessed 8/18.

Day 92

The story about the two steamboats is from www.sermoncentral. com. Accessed 2/17. "What Will You Give Up To Win?"

Day 93

The story about Jimmy Ellis the boxer is from www.sermoncentral. com. Accessed 4/18.

Day 94

The story about John Grisham is from www.preachingtoday.com. Accessed 9/15. "Novelist John Grisham's Road to Writing" from *Simplify*, Bill Hybels, Tyndale Press, 2014, page 40. And from www. wikipedia.org. Accessed 10/15.

Day 96

The adage about can-do people is from www.sermoncentral.com. Accessed 5/17. By John Stevens. Source unknown.
The story about the man trying out for the cross-country team is from www.sermoncentral.com. Accessed 5/17. Source: "Don't Lose Heart" sermon by Christopher Nerreau.

Day 97

The story about *The Andy Griffith Show* and Opie is from www. sermoncentral.com. Accessed 8/18. Information confirmed on Dailymotion. *The Andy Griffith Show* SO2E01_Opie and the Bully. Accessed 8/18.

Day 99

The story about Dave training for a 5K run is from www.sermoncentral. com. Accessed 3/18.